BUILD YOUR DREAMS

HOW TO MAKE A LIVING
DOING WHAT YOU LOVE

Alexis Irvin & Chip Hiden

RUNNING PRESS
PHILADELPHIA · LONDON

Books published by Running Press are available at special discounts for bulk
purchases in the United States by corporations, institutions, and other organizations.
For more information, please contact the Special Markets Department at the
Perseus Books Group, 2300 Chestnut Street, Suite 200, Philadelphia, PA 19103, or
call (800) 810-4145, ext. 5000, or e-mail special.markets@perseusbooks.com.

ISBN 978-0-7624-5038-1
Library of Congress Control Number: 2013935894

E-book ISBN 978-0-7624-5058-9

9   8   7   6   5   4   3   2   1
Digit on the right indicates the number of this printing

Designed by Joshua McDonnell
Edited by Cindy De La Hoz
Typography: Archer and Avenir

Running Press Book Publishers
2300 Chestnut Street
Philadelphia, PA 19103-4371

Visit us on the web!
www.runningpress.com

To anyone with a big idea and a little voice inside them saying, "Go!"

CONTENTS

THIS IS OUR STORY

What do you want to do with your life? That was the question burning in our minds after college graduation in 2009. Armed with two liberal arts degrees (Chip in history and Alexis in journalism), we faced an economic slump, a crushed job market, and the media's endless predictions of doom and gloom for young workers. The future loomed before us, foggy and uncertain. The pressure to get a job, earn money, and make our parents happy was intense. So, we did what we were supposed to do. We stuck to the traditional path and sent dozens of résumés out. We felt incredibly lucky when we found desk jobs after a month or so of searching.

The first few months on the job were exciting. We were young professionals—commuting to an office every morning, drinking coffee, having meetings, and most importantly, getting paid. But, after almost a year of pencil-pushing, it started to feel like something was missing. The initial excitement about work and the transition into adulthood faded. Work became a routine, an obligation. We were living for the weekends and working only for a paycheck.

We started to dread each workday—sitting in traffic for hours to go to a place we didn't really want to be, and being told we were too young for any meaningful responsibilities. As time dragged on, we tried to convince ourselves that the salary was worth it. But in the back of our minds, questions and doubts began to surface: Is this how some people feel every day when they wake up? Is this all there is to life?

We felt like we were on a path to a life we didn't want: working in the same office for forty years, building up a stack of worrisome bills, and putting off our dreams until retirement. For many, a steady, secure office job may be a dream come true. It just wasn't ours. We knew that we were lucky to even have jobs. But, for some reason life felt empty. We were cogs in a machine with no sense of calling or higher purpose. We wanted to leverage our privilege and our talents to do some good for the world, not languish our best years away in jobs we felt no passion for.

So, we came up with *the plan*.

Hatching Plans

One night out, we started talking about how we could bust out of our office-induced comas to figure out what we cared about. We decided to go on an epic U.S. road trip.

Our trek would take us from our hometown of Washington D.C., to the Great Lakes, through the Wild West, to the beaches of California, to roadhouses in Texas, to jazz clubs in New Orleans, and back home through the South. The road trip was the start of a good plan. But we realized that taking a vacation was not going to solve our problems with the office jobs. So, we made an addition to the road trip agenda. Along the way, we would film interviews with successful people who had chased their dreams and found work that they loved. We would collect their advice and anecdotes about discovering a passion, overcoming challenges, finding happiness, and making money. The goal was to make a movie that would compile the stories and encourage young people to chase their dreams.

THE ROAD TRIP

Equipped with a bare-bones budget, rations of Ramen Noodles, and a tiny red tent, we took the plunge. With just enough money for our trip, we left our jobs and hit the road. Our three-month journey took us coast-to-coast and introduced us to thirty different entrepreneurs, artists, activists, writers, nonprofit founders, producers, and athletes. These were people who were passionate, committed, and successful.

We met one of the original Latin Kings of Comedy in a chance encounter at a Louisville bar, toured Chicago's Museum of Science and Industry with a *Project Runway* fashion designer, chatted with an Olympic skier in Park City, Utah (home of the 2002 Winter Olympics), and sampled beer at 9 a.m. with the founder of the only craft brewery in New Orleans. Everyone we met with was brimming with energy. These were people who had found their place in the universe and had built careers that gave them a sense of purpose and meaning.

When we weren't filming people on our tiny Flip cameras, we were embracing life on the road and exploring every tourist attraction and roadside oddity we came across. We camped across the entire country and cooked food over an open fire. We learned to set up our tent in five minutes flat and to sleep outside in the rain, wind, and freezing cold. We narrowly escaped bears in South Dakota, a rogue alligator in Georgia, and a tow truck while sleeping in a Denny's parking lot. We stayed in a dirt-cheap hotel on the strip in Las Vegas, hiked the backwoods in Yosemite, and dipped our toes in the Great Salt Lake. It was the classic road trip experience.

Back Home

Once we came home, we spent eight months piecing together footage about our trip and everything we had learned. When it was done, we set up screenings of *The Dream Share Project* film at colleges and designed a workshop to help students discover and pursue their passions. We have since presented to thousands of young people across the country, working to empower them to pursue their dreams and reject the pressure to "play it safe." The response to *The Dream Share Project* has been overwhelmingly positive. After speaking with students all over the country about the challenges of dream-chasing, we wanted to expand on our message and write an in-depth manual for anyone looking to turn their dreams into reality. We wrote this book to guide you through the process of identifying and chasing your dreams.

WHY DREAM?

This book is for anyone who wants to pursue a life filled with passionate work. The tools in this book will help you identify your passions, commit to your goals, overcome obstacles, and start living your dreams.

Dreams are essential to progress. No one ever cured a disease, created a great work of art, or shook up the business world, without pursuing their dream. Successful men and women all throughout history had the courage to turn their big ideas into reality. You can too. Besides having a positive impact on others, a dream can make you happier in your daily life. Passionate people are happy people. If you want to look forward to going to work each day, then this book is for you.

It's not selfish or silly to want to love what you do for a living. We spend more time at work than we do with our families or friends, or on any other activity besides sleeping. Yet, millions of us spend the majority of our waking hours at work feeling miserable and unhappy. A recent CBS news poll found that 55 percent of Americans are dissatisfied with their jobs. Workers under the age of twenty-five expressed the greatest levels of dissatisfaction. According to the Families & Work Institute, 1/3 of the work force shows signs of depression. Even worse, passionless employees are unproductive. According to a study by the Hay Group, "offices with engaged employees were as much as 43 percent more productive" than those with unenthusiastic workers.

We have a National Dream Deficit on our hands, and it's bad for business.

The solution isn't complicated: Chase your dreams. Get happy. Perform better. Contribute to the greater good. We owe it to ourselves and the world to discover our passion and live up to our potential. Dreams help others, increase joy, revolutionize technology, create jobs, educate communities, improve society, fix the environment, and change the world. Failing to recognize and follow your dream is a waste of the precious gift of life. The clock is ticking. Do you want a life of grand

and passionate adventure? Or a life spent in the safe harbor? The choice is yours. Seize your destiny. Live the life you've always imagined. Start small. Start now.

But How?

How do I figure out what I am passionate about? How can I find or create my dream job? How do I get the money I need to chase my dream? What about my parents' expectations for my life? What happens if I fail?

These are the questions we all start with. These are the questions this book will answer.

WHAT TO EXPECT

We will guide you through all the stages of chasing a dream—from discovering or refining your passion, to dealing with challenges, to making a living doing what you love. This book will help you if:

- You have no idea what your dreams are.
- You have many passions, but can't decide the right one to pursue.
- You've always had a dream in mind but are scared to begin or don't know where to start.
- You have taken tentative steps towards your dream but need guidance on your next steps.

Chasing a dream is full of ups and downs. The highs are more gratifying than anything you've ever experienced. The lows are gut-wrenching. The road is often bumpy and covered in potholes. We hope you will use this book to avoid some of the most common roadblocks and seek out shortcuts to make your journey easier.

We have created a five-stage framework called D.R.E.A.M to help you find a passionate career:

Stage 1: Discover: your calling through reflection, analysis of your past, and exploration of six ways to test-drive a dream.

Stage 2: Research: the steps you need to take to reach your goal and overcome roadblocks.

Stage 3: Embark: on your journey by making a public commitment and financing your dream.

Stage 4: Adapt: your plan as you deal with challenges, loss of motivation, and rejection.

Stage 5: Maintain: your dream career by exploring multiple revenue streams and ways to give back.

The first three chapters of this book will show you how to discover your dream. We'll kick things off in chapter 1 by analyzing your childhood aspirations to find clues about your personality and predispositions. Then, we'll reflect on past experiences that shaped you.

In chapter 2 we'll continue to reflect by focusing on six topics that help illuminate your dream: interests, values, talents, environment, rewards, and current situation.

In chapter 3 you will differentiate between hobbies and your true passion and embark on six trial runs to put your interests to the test.

In chapter 4 we'll dismantle common roadblocks, such as doubtful parents and peers, fear of failure, and paralysis by analysis.

Once you've overcome your doubts, chapter 5 will teach you to make a step-by-step plan for achieving your dream. We'll provide twenty-five example step-by-step plans and research methods to help you create action items for your goals.

Chapter 6 helps you enact your plan with daily, incremental work. We'll show you how to balance your busy schedule and find gaps of time for dream work.

In chapter 7 you will slash expenses and beg, borrow, and barter to get your dream off the ground for cheap.

Chapter 8 explores ten fundraising sources, such as investors, loans, and crowdsourcing websites like kickstarter.com.

Chapter 9 provides tips for maintaining motivation through the daily drudgery of dream chasing. We'll help you overcome perfectionism and procrastination so you can cross the bridge from halfway to completion.

In chapter 10 you will launch your dream and embrace your inner salesperson. We'll show you how to build a brand, find your ideal customers, write a pitch, and publicize your work.

Once your work is out in the world, you open yourself up to rejection and criticism. In chapter 11 we'll teach you how to weather the storm, find your "rejection number," and develop the persistence needed to achieve your big break.

Finally, in chapter 12 we'll help you increase your impact and boost cash flow with new revenue streams. We'll show you how to build on your achievements, find your next project, and create lasting success.

HOW TO USE THIS BOOK

Each chapter contains journaling exercises and tasks to assist you in identifying and pursuing your dreams. We've developed these exercises based on our first-hand experience, as well as our interviews with successful dream-chasers, career counselors, and psychologists. You will need to keep a journal to write in and track your progress. Before you read any further, go get a notebook.

Writing assignments are embedded throughout each chapter—you can complete them as you come across them or after reading the entire chapter. Some of the exercises in the later chapters might be inapplicable the first time you read them. Bookmark them and come back when you're ready.

Our Promise: By the end of this book, you will have discovered your dream and have the tools to create a life filled with meaningful, passionate work.

We Believe

We are born dreamers. We are meant to chase our dreams.

Ignoring your dreams creates adverse effects for you and others. Don't waste your gifts.

The universe rewards those who commit to their dreams.

The greatest rewards follow the greatest challenges.

You can chase your dream without sacrificing a paycheck.

Dreams can come true with enough passion, adaptability, hard work, and risk-taking.

As we chase our dreams, we approach self-actualization and a fulfillment of our full potential.

Life is short. Don't waste another second. Now is the time to chase your dreams.

CHAPTER 1

DIG UP THE PAST

Look back to find your dream.

"Life can only be understood backwards; but it must be lived forwards."

—Søren Kierkegaard

When you're younger, it's easy to imagine a million different jobs you would be great at: teacher, movie star, or veterinarian. The sky's the limit. Then, as we grow up, we start to abandon or compromise our big dreams. "How am I ever going to become a professional pianist? That's a one-in-a-million shot. . . . Starting my own school would be too hard. Maybe I should just be a teacher at someone else's school. . . . I'm never going to make any money as an inventor. Maybe I should just apply to medical school."

Somewhere in the turmoil between adolescence and adulthood, we buy into the following advice: "It's time to grow up, get serious, and get a real job." So, we put aside childhood dreams and experiences, believing they have no relevance to our future. This is a mistake. Your past made you the person you are today. Don't shove it away. Even if your interests have changed, analysis of the past will unearth clues about your personality, motivations, and passions. Let's look at:

1. Childhood Aspirations
2. Discouragement from Dream Thieves
3. Transforming Hardship into Passion
4. Past Joys and Journeys
5. Your Media Inspirations

CHILDHOOD ASPIRATIONS

EXERCISE: What did you want to be when you grew up? (If you had lots of dreams, pick your favorite one.)

Painting a detailed picture of your childhood dream can help point out your enduring interests, skills you enjoy using, the environment you want to work in, the type of people you want to work with, your dominant personality traits, and your beliefs about the meaning of success.

Let's dissect an example childhood dream: Mike's dream was to be a marine biologist.

	Detail Your Dream	Mike's Answers	How Does This Translate to Today?
1.	Of all the possible dreams, why did you pick this one?	I was fascinated by sharks. I loved watching Discovery Channel's Shark Week.	Mike might still be interested in: sea life, animals, oceanography, environmental science, ecology, or conservation.
2.	In your dream job, what exactly were you doing?	Diving the ocean depths, filming sharks, and taking underwater photographs.	Mike might want his work to involve the following skills: swimming, scuba diving, filmmaking, photography, or storytelling.
3.	Where were you?	Deep underwater, surrounded by coral reefs and fish.	Mike may want to work near the water, live in a coastal region, work at an aquarium, or have a lakefront office.
4.	Who were you with?	I was with a small crew. I was the leader, camera-operator, and chief diver. Someone else was steering the boat. I had an assistant handling technology and research.	Mike should probably search for a job that lets him work with a small team. He should eventually seek a leadership role.
5.	What was the pinnacle of success in your dream?	To discover a new breed of shark, to have a show on Discovery Channel, and to lecture about marine biology at Harvard.	Mike seems to value knowledge, prestige, and teaching others. He should choose a career that will provide these rewards.

By asking these detailed questions about your childhood dreams, you can discover clues about your personality and preferences. Piecing these clues together will help you determine which career path to pursue.

EXERCISE: Answer these questions to examine your childhood dream.

Detail Your Dream

1. Of all the possible dreams, why did you pick this one?

_____

2. In your dream job, what exactly were you doing?

_____

3. Where were you?

_____

4. Who were you with?

_____

5. What was the pinnacle of success in your dream?

_____

How Does This Translate to Today?

1.

_____

2.

_____

3.

_____

4.

_____

5.

_____

DISCOURAGEMENT FROM DREAM THIEVES

Your childhood dream may have changed because new interests or hobbies took center stage. Or, your dream may have been stifled and snuffed out by a past discouragement. Was your childhood aspiration hijacked by one of the following dream thieves?

Bullies, Frenemies, and the Cool Kids: Sometimes we cast off a dream to fit in. Maybe your dreams of being a paleontologist were put to pasture when a playground bully made fun of your dinosaur T-shirt. You chickened out of ballet class after a friend called it stupid and boring. Or, none of your friends were interested in foreign affairs, so you kept your passion for international relations to yourself.

Authority Figure: Dreams can die when we are scared straight by the demigods of youth: parents, teachers, coaches, group leaders, tutors, a friend's parents, or older siblings. A crotchety English teacher didn't understand your futuristic story idea, so you quit penning your novel about Planet Gwarern and the Elvish Knights. You ditched the debate team after an intense critique of your performance by the coach. Your parents only encouraged the talents they deemed worthwhile—your dad ignored your A+ essays about Shakespeare, and instead, paid for you to take computer science classes each summer.

Personal Failure: Maybe your own trips, slips, and missteps derailed your dreams. You quit soccer after missing the last goal in a big match. You forgot your lines in the play and skipped auditions for the next production. Or, your first article for the school newspaper was heavily edited, and it discouraged you from writing another one.

Was your dream stolen from you? If so, you need to reclaim it or move on. Left to linger, old disappointments can sap your confidence and willingness to try new things. To move forward, forgive yourself for past failures, ditched dreams, and the resulting fallout. It doesn't matter that you missed a goal and quit ten years ago. All that matters is what you do today.

EXERCISE: Describe three or more moments when you felt discouraged by one of the dream thieves: a bully, frenemy, cool kid, authority figure, or past failure.

EXERCISE: Reclaim or move on. For each discouragement you listed above, complete one or more of the following exercises:

- Write a paragraph describing the discouragement or failure in all its gory, cringe-inducing detail. Then, rip the paper up, symbolically shredding the negativity surrounding this memory.
- Write a letter to your dream thief. "Dear Mom, it really infuriated me when you told me I wasn't a good enough dancer . . ." Destroy this letter once you're done to stop playing the blame game. You're in control from here on out.
- Try your dream again or plan a new risk that will give you back your confidence. Join a team, volunteer somewhere, talk to a stranger, or proudly wear your dinosaur T-shirt out on the town.

TRANSFORMING HARDSHIP INTO PASSION

Reflecting on the past can be difficult. Aside from dream thieves, your past might contain hardship, tragedy, and memories you've worked hard to bury. Many of us avoid reopening these old wounds in an attempt to shield ourselves from pain. However, for some, past tragedy can be a catalyst. It gives them a mission, something to fight for, and fills life with meaning and purpose. Can your past hardships inspire a dream for a better future? Kathy Eldon's twenty-two-year-old son Dan was stoned to death by a mob while working as a photojournalist for Reuters in Somalia in 1993. Kathy found a way to celebrate her son's life by starting the Creative Visions Foundation (CVF), which supports creative activists, like Dan, who use media to create positive social change. Since its inception, CVF has had a global impact, raising more than $11 million for creative activist projects in 195 countries to date.

Ocean Robbins is an adjunct professor of Peace Studies at Chapman University, a writer, and a speaker. Ocean and his wife have autistic twin sons. In an interview, Ocean told us, "My kids have so much joy in their life and so much joy in their hearts, but it's hard. It's difficult to try to make a difference in the world when sometimes, it feels like an accomplishment just to get through the day." Ocean's dreams of world peace have evolved to include raising awareness for autism with his writing and speaking engagements.

At the University of Tampa, we met a student named Hector Manley who lost both of his legs in a fire at age eleven. At twenty-two, Hector became the first double amputee to kayak the entire Mississippi River. In addition to rowing 2,500 miles in three months, Hector managed to raise nearly $50,000 dollars for the Wheelchair Foundation and Wounded Warriors. Hector told us his next goal is to climb Aconcagua, a 23,000-foot mountain in South America.

EXERCISE: What is a hardship that has affected you or a loved one? What are three ways you could fight back?

PAST JOYS AND JOURNEYS

On the other side of the coin, dreams can be inspired by happy memories and adventures. Traveling somewhere unfamiliar can birth fresh ideas and expose you to different ways of life. Many successful people have stumbled upon a brilliant idea while trekking the globe.

Howard Schultz was on a business trip to Milan, Italy, when he noticed that the coffee shops on every street corner were community-gathering points, where friends and business associates met. Today, Schultz is the CEO of Starbucks.

C. J. Proctor brought basketball to England after watching a game of hoops on a trip to Canada, where James Naismith had invented the game only a year earlier.

Mary Shelley based most of the action of *Frankenstein* in Geneva, Switzerland, where she had traveled as a young woman. During one visit, the rainy weather forced Mary and her friends indoors. They passed the time with ghost stories and discussions of new scientific experiments in galvanism, the contraction of muscles stimulated by electricity. The creepy settings, spooky tales, and scientific discussion sparked the idea for the story of a monster born in a laboratory.

Travel is a great, albeit expensive, source of inspiration for dreams. Not all of us have had a chance to vacation in Switzerland. But, inspiration can also strike with local travel: a trip to a nearby town you have never visited, a journey to a store or museum, or hiking in a new-to-you state park. Anytime you leave the familiar behind, you give yourself an opportunity to be inspired and develop fresh ideas.

EXERCISE: Reflect on one or more travel experiences you've had—a school trip, vacation, a work trip, or a time you went somewhere new. Answer the following:

- What inspired you?
- What surprised you?
- Did you meet or see any interesting people?
- Did you get any new ideas after your experience?

EXERCISE: This week, plan a day trip to somewhere you've never been before. Take a notebook and jot down ideas, observations, or descriptions of any interesting characters you see or meet along the way.

YOUR MEDIA INSPIRATIONS

What sections of the bookstore do you always find yourself in? What magazines do you constantly pick up, year after year? What films or TV shows shaped your youth? You can learn a lot about your career aspirations by examining recurring book, film, and television choices. What topics do you keep coming back to? Why?

Scott Shuffitt loved the movie *The Big Lebowski* so much that he created *Lebowski Fest*, an annual multi-city festival that celebrates all things related to the Coen brothers' cult classic. At the event, attendees dress like characters from the film, watch the movie together, and then go bowling. Scott and his partner sell tickets, sponsorships, merchandise, and White Russian drinks at the event to bring in revenue. Scott's favorite movie led to his dream job. When has a piece of media or an experience touched, influenced, or inspired you?

EXERCISE: Answer the following questions
- Who are some of your favorite fictional (book or film) heroes and heroines? What do you admire the most about them?
- What are your favorite books, TV shows, and movies?
- Does a particular genre (true crime, comedy, cooking) interest you?
- What websites do you love to visit during your free time?
- What type of information do you find yourself researching a lot?
- What do the above answers teach you about yourself and your dreams?

SUMMARY POINTS

- Looking back and creating a detailed vision of your childhood dream can provide clues about your personality, preferences, and interests. One of these clues may point the way to your dream job.

- Past discouragements from dream thieves need to be processed so you can move on.

- Hardships and tragedy can be a catalyst for a dream.

- Traveling and exploring the unfamiliar exposes you to different ways of life and sparks ideas.

- Your favorites among books, films, stories, and other media indicate your passions.

CHAPTER 2:

MIRROR, MIRROR

Use self-reflection to define your dream.

"Know thyself"

—Plato

Self-understanding is the cornerstone and foundation we build dreams on. Reflection clears out the mental clutter of other people telling you what to think and how to act. Let's reflect on the following topics to clarify your goals:

1. Interests
2. Values
3. Talents
4. Work Environment
5. Rewards
6. Your Current Situation

Some of us think reflection is a practice reserved for meditative monks and therapists. "I'm not the contemplative type. . . . Reflection is a waste of time. . . . Why write in a diary when I could go *do* something?" Push aside your skepticism. The best and brightest practice daily reflection. British entrepreneur Sir Richard Branson has dozens of notebooks filled with his reflections, lists, and ideas. Writer Stephen King goes for a daily walk to collect his thoughts. Painter Frida Kahlo reportedly wrote in a diary every day. There are many ways to practice daily reflection. Maybe mulling over a recent business trip in the shower reveals an urge to move somewhere new. Perhaps keeping a diary will show you it's time to end your current relationship and start fresh. Or, daily meditation could expose a desire to change careers. Regular reflection sows the seeds for new plans and dreams. It doesn't matter how you self-reflect, it just matters that you do. Try some of the following:

Write in a journal

Meditate

Pray

Go for a walk, run, swim, or bike ride

Use your shower or bath time to think

Walk your pet

Record voice memos on your phone during your commute

EXERCISE: Many people say great ideas and moments of reflection come to them in the shower. This week, keep a shower idea log: After you get out of the shower, jot down any insights or brilliant ideas you had. For example, *Monday: Someone should make Froot Loops ice cream. Could I make it?*

EXERCISE: This week, commit to fifteen minutes a day of quiet time and self-reflection. Start now: put down the book, turn off all electronics, and sit still. Let your thoughts wander. Be sure to jot down any ideas you want to remember.

REFLECTION TOPIC #1:

INTERESTS

What are the activities you would do all day, every day, for free? What are the topics that make you lean forward in your chair and raptly pay attention? What do you have an endless appetite for? What fascinates or intrigues you? What do you want to learn more about? What activities give you a feeling of flow—you are so immersed that you don't notice time passing, you feel totally in the zone?

Your answers to the questions above are the key to discovering your passion. The topics we love are the perfect springboards for future dreams. Your interests fire you up. When you have an intrinsic love for something, it's easy to brainstorm innovative ideas, produce high quality work, and maintain motivation.

Connecting Interests to Career

Don't succumb to the belief that your interests can't become paid work. With enough creativity, hard work, and flexibility, you can make money doing almost anything. There are six different Career Lenses, or ways to make money in our society:

1. Business
2. Creative
3. Hands-on
4. Scientific/Research
5. Social/Political
6. Teaching

Viewing your interest through one or more of these Career Lenses helps you brainstorm possible ways to earn money. For example:

My Interest: Food

Business: Open a restaurant, run a catering company, open a grocery store, work for a food supplier, invent a brand of food, do marketing for a food company, do food sales, start a farmer's market, organize a restaurant week.

Creative: Write restaurant reviews, take pictures of food for magazines, paint food still lifes, start a food blog, create menus, make a film about food, write a book about your experience in the food-service industry.

Hands-on: Be a chef, work as a farmer, be a butcher, bake bread, catch fish, brew and bottle beverages, be a recipe developer.

Scientific/Research: Test food products for safety, work on nutrition labels, organize clinical trials with food, research health benefits/drawbacks of food products, research best practices in farming, write reports on food processing, analyze crop yield.

Social/Political: Work as a lobbyist for organic farmers, create a law for food safety, organize food donations, start a campaign for healthier school lunches, start a nonprofit soup kitchen.

Teaching: Teach others to cook, teach sustainable farming, teach crop cycles, teach youth about nutrition, host community classes, create a mentoring program for young farmers.

EXERCISE: Plug your interest into the Six Career Lenses to brainstorm every possible career related to your interest. Feel free to repeat this exercise with more than one interest!

Combining Interests

If you have lots of interests, try to combine two or three into a new career path. Nicolle Fuller combined her love of science and art into a career as a scientific illustrator. She tested out her passion by taking classes at UC Santa Cruz Science Illustration Program. Later, she earned a job at the National Science Foundation, and eventually started her own scientific illustration company, Sayo-Art LLC.

Musician Harvey Reid has had a lifelong love of mathematics. He applies math to his musical career by arranging logical melodies and harmonies, troubleshooting 16-channel sound systems, and creating efficient touring schedules and budgets.

Jim Shmerling knew he wanted to work with children but also felt passionate about law, medicine, and business. He is now the CEO and president of Children's Hospital Colorado.

EXERCISE: If you have multiple interests, write down three career paths that would combine them.

REFLECTION TOPIC #2:

VALUES

Your dream career should be a representation of your values. Your values are the core, defining principles and ethics that inform how you should live and work.

EXERCISE: Answer the following questions to determine your values. What do you care about most? When do you feel proud of yourself? What traits do these proud moments demonstrate? What kind of person do you want to be? How do you want others to describe you?

EXERCISE: What are your top 10 values? Answer this quickly, based off your gut reaction. Choose from this list or make up your own:

Honesty	Decisiveness	Ambition	Peace
Bravery	Contentment	Frankness	Popularity
Control	Excitement	Generosity	Resilience
Duty	Entertainment	Harmony	Realism
Structure	Adventure	Assurance	Simplicity
Knowledge	Consistency	Humility	Power
Accuracy	Articulateness	Adaptability	Traditionalism
Charm	Balance	Humor	Security
Commitment	Boldness	Cleverness	Creativity
Dependability	Belonging	Independence	Spontaneity
Wisdom	Compassion	Kindness	Service
Discovery	Dignity	Longevity	Trustworthiness
Economy	Energy	Optimism	Variety
Affluence	Fairness	Organization	Cooperation
Endurance	Loyalty	Originality	Equality

Connecting Values and Career

Work that doesn't line up with your values can lead to a creeping sense of dissatisfaction, making you feel like an imposter in your own skin. Alex was a comedian by night and a miserable salesman by day. John was the heir to a multi-million dollar company that violated his ethical beliefs about environmental justice. Danielle made a profitable living selling advertisements for other companies, while at night she secretly yearned to create and market her own product. For all three, there was conflict between values and work. A lot of people try to mold themselves and their values to fit a certain job, organization, or culture. That's a lost cause. Work should be an extension of your values, not someone else's.

Today, Alex is a full-time comedian, John is a celebrated author and speaker on environmental sustainability, and Danielle runs an organic nut butter business and a charity organization that helps feed hungry kids. By realigning their actions and career with what they cared about, these dreamers created lives that feel congruent and harmonious. They are making a living doing what they love.

EXERCISE: Brainstorm three or more careers that align with your values.

REFLECTION TOPIC #3:

TALENTS

Work doesn't need to be an uphill struggle. Do what you're good at. What are your inherent skills and gifts? What comes easily to you? What can you contribute? There's a job for every skill:

Leading	Organizing
Data-crunching	Cleaning
Creating	Drawing
Problem solving	Buying
Building	Managing
Project or event planning	Designing
Writing	Talking
Researching	Decorating
Experimenting	Baking
Lobbying	Inventing
Campaigning	Motivating
Teaching	Listening
Selling	Asking questions
Sewing	Making people laugh

EXERCISE: What are you amazing at? Make a list.

Connecting Talents and Career

One day in P. E. class, Jon discovered his natural talent. He could climb. He was the fastest in his class to shimmy to the top of the ropes course. After that day, Jon began spending every free minute rock climbing. In college he led climbing trips up the Arizona mountains. Once he graduated, he became a rock-climbing instructor and youth coach at the local Rocks and Ropes gym. You can make a living using your talents too. To start, ask yourself: who will pay you to do what you're good at?

EXERCISE: What are your five favorite skills to use? Brainstorm five jobs that would use these skills frequently.

REFLECTION TOPIC #4:

WORK ENVIRONMENT

Where do you want to work? Your ideal workspace might be outside, a lavish office, your desk at home, on the road, abroad, a studio, a rehearsal space, an athletic field, a laboratory, a conference room, or an auditorium. What career will give you access to the places you love? Your work environment also includes the people you work with. Some of us relish the thought of spending hours alone in a room on a laptop, while others thrive off the energy of working with a team. Consider your preferences for workmates when you think about your dream job.

EXERCISE: Create a vision for your ideal workspace by answering the following questions:

• What would your dream workspace look like?

_____

_____

• Ideally, who would you work with? A small team, a large team, with a partner, or alone?

_____

_____

• Would you like to lead, follow, or have everyone be equal?

_____

_____

• What type of culture does your ideal work place have? Is it corporate, casual, fast-paced, or slow-paced?

_____

_____

• What is your ideal schedule?

_____

_____

• What is your ideal dress code?

_____

_____

• If you are employed, how does your current work environment compare to your ideal work environment?

_____

_____

REFLECTION TOPIC #5:

REWARDS

Rewards are the fun part of work, the sweet stuff we get once we put the time and effort in. Rewards are essential to great work and innovation. They make us want to move, create, and get things done. When searching for your dream, keep in mind the rewards you hope to reap in the future, such as:

Intrinsic enjoyment of the work

Money

Personal accomplishment

Receiving recognition and praise

Giving recognition and praise

Fame or prestige

Creating a product

Being creative

Helping others

Improving or impacting a community

New challenges, variety in your work

Career advancement

Opportunity to learn

Opportunity to lead

Connecting Rewards and Career

Letting others influence the rewards you pursue causes inner confusion: Why isn't the chance to spearhead a project making you jump for joy? Why isn't your big office making you any happier? Why aren't we satisfied with what we have? Your reward system is unique to you. Don't let parents, media, or a work culture belittle or dictate the rewards you seek. Prioritizing the rewards you crave most can illuminate the path to your dream job. For example:

If your top reward is **giving praise and recognition to others**, then maybe you should be a leader, coach, or teacher.

If your top reward is **creating a finished product**, you might enjoy being an inventor, artist, or web developer.

If your top rewards are **helping others and autonomy**, you could try building a community program, starting your own nonprofit, or becoming a social entrepreneur.

EXERCISE: What are the rewards you care about most? Create a prioritized list of rewards, from most important (1) to least important (10).

1. _____   6. _____

2. _____   7. _____

3. _____   8. _____

4. _____   9. _____

5. _____   10. _____

EXERCISE: Reflect on three times you were rewarded in the past. It could be the time you first got paid, helped someone in need, or accomplished something you had long hoped for. Describe these experiences and how you felt about the reward you were given.

1. _____
_____

2. _____
_____

3. _____
_____

EXERCISE: Brainstorm three careers that provide the rewards you care about most.

1. _____
_____

2. _____
_____

3. _____
_____

REFLECTION TOPIC #6:

YOUR CURRENT SITUATION

Are you happy with your current work situation? Reflection is a critical tool for pinpointing and then fixing work-related problems and shortcomings. We can't begin to solve our dilemmas until we put a name, face, or place to the trouble. For example, maybe your past few journal entries have revealed:

I'm jealous of Cindy's Parisian business trip.

My commute is unbearable.

I wish I could work for the advertising department—it seems so much more creative.

Once you've identified the issue at hand, you can take action. Listen to your inner voice to brainstorm possible solutions. For example:

To satisfy my Francophilia: I'm going to research the cost of renting an apartment in Paris, take a class on the French Revolution, or plan a trip to the French bakery with a friend.

To cut back on commuting: I'm going to ask to telecommute two days a week, take the commuter bus, or start a car pool with coworkers.

To explore advertising jobs: I'll learn more about what the advertising department really does, have lunch with one of its members, or ask for an informational interview with the department head.

The resolutions you come up with should be in proportion to the problem you are facing. If you are absolutely miserable, a big change is needed. If something is just a pet peeve, deal with it quickly and move on. Keep Occam's razor in mind—the simplest solution is usually the right one.

EXERCISE: Write down three problems that are bothering you right now. Next, brainstorm a solution for each. Set a deadline for solving each problem, then take action.

EXERCISE: Use the following journal prompts to reflect on your current situation. Pick a topic that strikes you and write at least a page.

1. What's making me happy right now?
2. I had an idea about . . .
3. I just noticed _____ and it's making me feel . . .
4. Where do I want to go?
5. In five years I want to be . . .
6. In ten years I want to be . . .
7. In twenty years I want to be . . .
8. In fifty years I want to be . . .
9. In a hundred years I want to be remembered as . . .
10. Recently I was really inspired by . . .
11. I need a big change. I think it should be . . .
12. I'm ready to take _____ to the next level. To do that I think I should . . .
13. I'm feeling really nervous about . . .
14. I'm feeling really excited about . . .
15. Lately, I've been wanting to . . .
16. If I had all the money in the world I would . . .
17. I need to let _____ go.
18. I'm ready to start _____ more.
19. I've been feeling very anxious about . . .
20. I want to focus on _____ now.
21. What is making me unhappy right now?
22. I've been feeling like I should . . .
23. I have been avoiding . . .
24. I wish I could be more like . . .
25. If I could buy five things right now I would buy . . .
26. I really have the urge to work on . . .
27. I want to change _____ habit.
28. I'm feeling very overwhelmed because . . .
29. I really admire _____ because . . .
30. If I could do something crazy today I would . . .

SUMMARY POINTS:

- Self-reflection is essential to discovering your dream. Establish a habit of daily reflection to keep track of new ideas. Without daily reflection we lose sight of our goals, our true feelings, and ourselves.

- Focus your reflection on six topics: values, interests, skills, work environment, rewards, and your current situation.

- Your career should align with your ethics and core beliefs.

- Creative brainstorming and the Six Career Lenses will show you how your interests and hobbies can become paid work.

- Do what you are good at. Reflect on your skills, then seek work that lets you shine.

- Create a vision for your ideal workplace. Seek the rewards you crave.

- Reflect on your current situation. Pinpoint your problems. Determine a solution. Take action.

CHAPTER 3:
CRACK A
FEW EGGS

Use trial runs to hone in on your dream.

"I'll try anything once, twice if I like it,
three times to make sure."

—Mae West

Once you've identified a potential dream through reflection, it's time to put it to the test. Let's explore six trial runs you can do to decide if an interest is worth further pursuit:

1. Volunteer
2. Job Shadow
3. Classes
4. Clubs
5. Interning
6. Start a Project

Trial runs are low-cost, low commitment, and efficient. They quickly teach you what you love, what you hate, and what you're just so-so about through actual experiences.

EXERCISE: Pick an interest for your trial runs. Make a list of the top five interests you want to explore further. Begin with #1 as you start your trial runs. Or use the interest you chose for the Six Career Lenses exercise in chapter 2.

A quick disclaimer:

Certain factors can negatively skew your evaluation of a trial run. The bumper-to-bumper commute made you loathe your volunteer gig. The president at a club meeting droned on and on, infatuated with the sound of his own voice. The law lost its luster after you shadowed an attorney working out of her cluttered and cramped home office.

One trial run is not indicative of an entire field or profession. Don't write off an industry because of a scatterbrained boss, wonky work environment, or an unbearable trek to your trial run.

TRIAL RUN METHOD #1:

VOLUNTEER

When Adrianne Prettyman first moved to New York, she supported herself as a corporate event planner. In her free time, she pursued her interest in animal rights by volunteering with the Farm Sanctuary Advocacy Campaign Team. She participated in outreach activities: leafleting, staffing benefit concerts, and coordinating the NYC Walk for Farm Animals. While volunteering, Adrianne established key connections with leaders in the activist community. Through networking, she was eventually offered her dream job as the program manager for The Seed, an organization that promotes veganism through events in New York City.

How to Find a Volunteer Opportunity

- *idealist.org:* This site offers opportunities in every state in the U.S. and worldwide.
- *volunteermatch.org:* The site lists nearly 75,000 opportunities all over the country.
- *serve.gov and volunteer.gov:* These offer opportunities at the local, state, and federal level.
- *scistarter.com:* This site specializes in science/research, with opportunities like SKYWARN (help meteorologists gather real-time weather data), the ShaRk Project (conduct simple chemistry experiments), Bat Detective (help scientists classify bat calls), and thousands of others.
- *ProBono.net:* This legal volunteering site provides opportunities for pro bono attorneys, law professors, students, and social service advocates. The site is organized by geographic region and practice area.
- *Political Volunteering:* Volunteer for a local politician by searching the websites of your state and local governments for lists of officials and their contact information. Or, seek out opportunities by joining a local political club.
- *Research Locally:* Are there any upcoming local events that relate to your interest? Contact the event organizers and ask to volunteer.

Tips to Keep in Mind

Take a flexible approach and search for opportunities that will give you experience for the job you want. Interested in working as a clinical psychologist? Consider volunteering with the Suicide Crisis Hotline or an after school program for underserved youth. Expect to do menial tasks—clean a closet, hand out flyers, or make phone calls. After getting your foot in the door, you can seek a leadership role. If you feel underutilized, work with the person in charge to create your own tasks and projects. Treat everyone you meet at work, events, and fundraisers as potential mentors or, future employers.

EXERCISE: Evaluate your volunteer experience by answering the following questions:

- What was the environment like?
- What did you like about this experience?
- What did you dislike about this experience?
- Do you have ideas for how work could be done more effectively?
- What tasks were you good at?
- What tasks were you not good at?
- What new skills did you pick up?
- Who did you meet?
- How did this experience help you?
- Do you want to explore this type of work further?

TRIAL RUN METHOD #2:

JOB SHADOW

Job shadowing is when you follow a professional on-the-job to learn about their daily duties. After graduating college, Jennifer Turliuk decided to explore her interest in entrepreneurship by shadowing the start-up kings and queens of Silicon Valley. She picked up the phone and secured shadowing experiences with companies like Kiva, Launchrock, Dojo, Causes (started by Sean Parker of Napster notoriety), and Ashoka (a nonprofit that supports entrepreneurship). Her goal was to dip her toe in and get a taste of each company. She stayed with each organization for a few days, helping out wherever she could. After shadowing, Jennifer realized she wanted to start her own business. Her approach to discovering her dream was "much cheaper than an MBA, which conventional wisdom says is needed to figure out your business passion."

How to Find a Job Shadow

To start, ask your family, friends, counselors, or teachers to refer you to a professional to shadow. Or, cold call and e-mail a professional doing something you want to do. Be sure to explain the concept of job shadowing. Some people might not know what it is. Don't ask for too much of their time. Start small, with a request for a few hours and let them know you are willing to help out. Don't be afraid to flatter—let them know why you admire them.

Sample E-mail for a Shadowing Experience

Dear Ms. Carter,

I am a junior business major and considering a career as a restaurant owner. I love your restaurant and had a great experience planning my mom's 50th birthday there last spring. I am writing to request a job shadow experience.

If possible, I would like to follow you around for an hour or two to learn what being a restaurant owner is all about. My goal is to see what the daily responsibilities and challenges of the job are. I'm willing to help out in any way I can.

I really admire the work you do and I would love to get your advice. I am available at any time that is convenient to you. I look forward to hearing from you.

Sincerely,

Chip

In addition to cold calling, you can reach out to a local branch of a professional organization to ask for a shadowing experience. There are groups for most professions such as the American Marketing Association, the American Society of Animal Science, and Fashion Group International, to name a few. Also, national Job Shadow Day is in early February. See if any local organizations are participating.

If you can't find someone in your town, consider virtual job shadowing. Jobshadow.com has video interviews with a variety of professionals: an iOS app developer, a freelance journalist, a sous chef, a conservation officer at the San Diego zoo, a poetry editor, and a record producer, among many others.

Tips to Keep in Mind

Don't shadow a disgruntled worker. Seek out someone who is passionate and successful. Your shadow experience should expose you to their work environment and day-to-day responsibilities, so don't just meet in a coffee shop. Remember to be flexible about who you shadow. In other words, be content shadowing a county council member if your Senator's office doesn't respond. Make yourself available at a date and time that works best for them. You're asking for a favor, so make it as convenient as possible. While you are shadowing, here are some questions you should ask:

- What are the responsibilities of your job?
- What is most rewarding about the job?
- What is most stressful or challenging?
- How did you get started?
- What are the steps to getting this job?
- Are there any special skills I need to obtain?
- If you're comfortable talking about it, what is the compensation for a job like this?
- Is there anything you wish you knew before you started?

Be sure to follow up with a thank you e-mail or handwritten note!

EXERCISE: After shadowing someone, answer the following questions:

- How did you feel about the day-to-day, possibly less glamorous, work of this profession?
- Did you like the work environment? Why or why not?
- What surprised you about this experience?
- What new things did you learn?
- Would you want to do something similar to this job? Why or why not?

TRIAL RUN METHOD #3:

CLASSES

In Iowa we met student entrepreneur Mokotsi Rukundo, creator of the CorNroc food cart. While attending the University of Iowa, Mokotsi started selling spicy corn-on-the-cob at football tailgates. He wanted to expand his operation, so he took classes at the entrepreneurial center on campus to develop a business plan. With the help of his professors, Mokotsi launched a profitable food cart business in downtown Iowa City. His zesty corn-on-the-cob has become iconic.

How to Find Classes

Taking a class doesn't have to mean going back to school full time. There are lots of other options: intensive one-day classes, seminars, semester-long options at a professional center, or auditing at a community college or university. Look for classes offered by local organizations like your local council on the arts, a nearby cooking school, or a gym. You can also educate yourself online. Use openculture.com to search for online classes or browse the web for consulting and coaching services offered by industry veterans. One of the best free educational resources available is iTunesU, which offers thousands of free podcast lectures from top universities and experts.

Tips to Keep in Mind

Teachers aren't perfect. Before enrolling, read reviews online, ask other classmates about their experiences, or speak with the professor to be sure it's a good fit. Education can be pricey, so be prepared to drop some cash on a class. Don't waste your time and money once you've signed up. Get involved. Sit up front where you can see the teacher, turn off your phone, and participate in discussions and projects.

EXERCISE: After taking a class, answer the following questions:

• What did you learn?
• Did you enjoy the subject matter and would you like to learn even more?
• What projects or assignments did you enjoy most?
• What parts of the class did you dislike?
• Did you meet anyone you'd like to work with again?
• Did you like the teacher?
• How can you apply what you learned in this class to future opportunities?

TRIAL RUN METHOD #4:

CLUBS

Writer, actor, and producer Jay Chandrasekhar, started a club in college for improvised sketch comedy with his fraternity brothers. Jay shelled out the cash for a digital camera and the group began making short videos. After college, the shorts grew longer and the group had an idea for a feature-length spoof about highway patrolmen: *Super Troopers*. Later they followed up with another smash hit, *Beerfest*. The Broken Lizard comedy troupe started as a college club and grew into a comedy powerhouse. Jay and the gang have gone on to produce, direct, write, and act in dozens of film and TV projects.

How to Find a Club

Look for club advertisements at schools, college campuses, town halls, professional centers, stores (like jam sessions at the local music shop), coffee shops, or anywhere there's a community bulletin board. Meetup.com lists clubs in your area for everything from Buddhism to sailing. Or, if there are no clubs for what you want, create your own like Jay did. Post a flyer in places where like-minded individuals would look, create a group on Facebook and meetup.com, and ask your friends to spread the word.

Tips to Keep in Mind

Keep an eye out for club politics. Anytime people organize, there will be some hierarchy, factions, or in-house bickering. Your time is precious. Don't put up with disorganized discussions or endless, agenda-less meetings. Make sure to ask about the level of commitment before making your membership official, kicking in dues, or volunteering for a project.

EXERCISE: After at least two club meetings, answer the following:

- How did it feel to be around like-minded people? Inspiring? Engaging? Competitive?
- How do the group's objectives align with your own?
- What have you accomplished or learned?
- So far, what has been the most fun?
- How could this club help you?
- Who did you meet?
- Do you have any ideas or projects to suggest to the club?

TRIAL RUN METHOD #5:

INTERNING

Raelle Myrick-Hodges wanted to pursue her love for theater but didn't have the money for a top-tier drama school. "Instead of going the education route, I made a list of all the theaters, directors, and playwrights I liked. Then, I interned for two years for free. I was pretty broke, but I loved it. I seriously think I have the best friends in the world—they fed and housed me for free as I was interning," she said. Raelle is now the Artistic Director of Brava Theater for Women in the Arts in San Francisco.

How to Find and Win an Internship

You've probably heard most of this before. If you're in school, visit your career services office, which should have a database of internships and employers. Or, look online, join e-mail listservs, and check out resources like internmatch.com and the internship section of idealist.org. Aim high. What sounds like an awesome place to work? Read up on the company and call their internship coordinator.

When applying, use your common sense and take care of the basics. Triple-proofread your résumé and cover letter and don't forget to secure the privacy settings on your social media accounts.

Research in-depth before the interview. Skimming a company's website for twenty minutes won't cut it. If you really want this internship, do your homework: What is this company known for? Have they been in the news lately? Who is the leadership? What is their background? Who are the competitors? What are this company's popular products or services? Do you use them? Are there any industry trends that affect the company? What could you contribute to this company? Bring a few new ideas to the table. For example, I have an idea for tracking the return on investment of your social media marketing, I'd like to start a daily blog, or I would love to plan an event to raise awareness for the company.

Don't hit snooze on your alarm the morning of an interview, get rid of your limp-wristed or bone-crushing handshake, and make sure your threads match the company culture. (Chip once wore a three-piece suit to an interview at a punk rock music venue. He did not get the internship.)

Tips to Keep in Mind

Applying for internships can be as competitive as applying for a real job. Don't let the rigorous application process mislead you. Many internships sound glamorous but require a good deal of grunt work, personal errands for your supervisor, and envelope stuffing.

Lower your expectations about parlaying your internship into a paid gig. In 2011, the National Association of College and Employers asked employers how many interns they ended up converting into paid employees. Out of the employers who responded, 58 percent offered jobs to interns. More drastically, research by the Partnership for Public Service shows that less than 7 percent of federal interns are converted to government jobs.

Before accepting an internship, think about how much it will cost you to commute, pay for lunch, and pony up for parking. Weigh the time and money required for this internship versus the potential benefits. If there's no stipend, you shouldn't be required to work full-time hours. Create a schedule with your internship coordinator that allows you to work a part-time job to pay the bills. Never let an internship break the bank.

The biggest perk of internships is connections and résumé-building. Ask for a letter of recommendation a week or two before the end of your internship. You may be able to leverage this letter into a paying job in the future.

EXERCISE: After an internship, answer the following questions:

- What tasks did you enjoy?
- What tasks did you dislike?
- Did you like or dislike the work environment? Why?
- Did you like or dislike the organizational structure? Why?
- How many people did you work with? Did you like or dislike the size of the organization?
- Who was your supervisor? What did you think of their leadership style?
- Who did you meet that could help you in the future?
- Would you want to do the job you saw someone else doing?
- What did you learn about your personality as you engaged with others?
- What skills did you learn or improve?
- What was the worst thing about the experience?
- What was the best thing about the experience?
- Is this a career option you want to explore further or rule out?

TRIAL RUN METHOD #6:

START A PROJECT

As a kid, Louis Black and his friend Leonard Maltin loved taking the subway into New York City to binge on B-movie matinees and buttery popcorn. Later on in college, Louis and some pals organized weekly movie screenings and campus film festivals to highlight their favorites in underrated cinema. These college projects were the first steps in Louis's successful career as a festival organizer. Years later, Louis and a group of venue owners and promoters started a much larger festival, South by Southwest, which now draws around 200,000 attendees each year.

How to Find Your Project

You don't always need a structured internship, the hierarchy of a club, or a formal education to gain experience. You can take matters into your own hands. Choose a project that sounds fun and challenging and bring it to life:

Launch a website or start a blog

Make a short video

Write and submit an article

Write a business plan

Make, bake, or create something to sell

Organize an event

Write a short screenplay, novella, book proposal, or play

Record a song on your laptop

Conduct an experiment

Sketch a schematic or algorithm for an invention

Offer your service to someone—tutoring, de-cluttering, haircut, or graphic design

Plan a small-scale campaign

Fundraise for a cause

Make a podcast or radio show

Tips to Keep in Mind

Keep it low budget. Your first project shouldn't empty your piggy bank. Use materials, people, places, products, or services that are free or cheap. If possible, get partners. It's easier to stay motivated and accountable when others are involved. Don't get caught up in endless revising and polishing. This is a small-scale project, not a masterpiece. Stick to a deadline.

EXERCISE: After working on a project, answer the following:

- Why did you take on this particular project?
- What skills did you gain?
- What did you enjoy most?
- What did you enjoy least?
- What surprised you?
- Did you work with anyone? How was that experience?
- If you were to do a similar project in the future, what would you do differently?
- Do you want to do another project like this or move on?
- Could this project grow into something bigger? How?

SUMMARY POINTS:

- The trial runs you can use to explore a potential passion are volunteering, shadowing, joining a club, taking a class, interning, and starting a project.

- Trial runs are never a waste of time as long as you learn something.

- Evaluation of your experiences is just as important as the experience itself. Always take a mental inventory of what you gained.

- Don't judge an industry based on one trial run. Seek out multiple avenues to explore an interest.

CHAPTER 4

THE MONSTERS UNDER THE BED

What mental roadblocks are holding you back?

"When a resolute young fellow steps up to the great bully, the world, and takes him boldly by the beard, he is often surprised to find it comes off in his hand, and that it was only tied on to scare away the timid adventurers."

—Ralph Waldo Emerson

Just like the monster under the bed, our doubts make us run back to our comfort zone and hide under the covers. We want to chase our dream, but we can't stop fretting over our fears. "I don't have the talent to pull this off. . . . I'll probably end up broke. . . . Everyone will make fun of me if I fail. . . . There are tons of people already doing what I want to do and I'll never be as successful as them."

Mental roadblocks are natural and we all suffer from them in one way or another. Let's explore and dismantle eight common roadblocks:

1. Seeking Approval from Parents or Loved Ones
2. Fear of Failure
3. Fear of Giving Up Security
4. Your Inner Critic
5. Believing Your Dream Is Silly, Selfish, or Frivolous
6. Thinking Your Dream Is Unoriginal
7. Hero Worship
8. Paralysis by Analysis

ROADBLOCK #1:

SEEKING APPROVAL FROM PARENTS OR LOVED ONES

"Parents aren't interested in justice; they're interested in peace and quiet."

—Bill Cosby

Picture This: You work up the courage to tell a loved one about your big idea. Instead of encouragement and smiles, your words are met with frowns and disparaging questions. You feel discouraged, dejected, and infuriated by their lack of support.

The Root Causes: Growing up, we are taught to seek approval from our parents and authority figures. As you develop your own worldview and opinions, there's bound to be a clash between what you think is best and what your loved ones want for you.

The people closest to you will have the most reservations about your dreams. Why? They love you and want to spare you from unstable finances, rejection, and hardship. Or, they may have another plan for you, like taking over the family business, going to law school, or applying for the same job they have. There might also be a generational gap—imagine a young Mark Zuckerberg trying to explain the idea for Facebook to his grandma.

Jealousy can poison your conversation with loved ones as well. Why should you get to chase your dream when your parents slaved away for twenty years to feed, clothe, house, and educate you? If you want to pursue something you love, it can force your parents or peers to question their own career choices. Did they not have the means to chase their own dream? Are they satisfied with life? Do they want to make their own career change?

How to Deal

Not everyone will agree with your dream. For people pleasers, this can be tough. We want to appease our parents and make our families and friends proud. But we also want to stop playing it safe and climb out from under the covers to see what the world has to offer. Everyone needs to rebel at some point; every bird eventually grows too big to stay in the nest.

To make the conversation with your loved ones go as smoothly as possible, wait until you have a well-researched plan, a budget, and a back-up plan for your dream. (We'll help you make a step-by-step plan in chapter 5 and help you save and raise funds in chapters 7 and 8). Once you have a plan, commit and don't flip-flop too much. Loved ones can grow weary and worried if you keep changing your mind every month. Like the little boy who cried wolf, soon your words will have no weight.

When you share your dream with a loved one, approach the conversation like a court case, and present evidence that success is possible. Provide examples of how others are earning a living doing something similar to your dream. As you make your case, keep in mind that the best way to earn support is through actions, not words. If possible, show your loved ones a physical product that you have put real work into—a portfolio, business plan, or website you built.

Another way to get loved ones to buy in to your dreams is to include them, ask for their help, or give them a job to do. Can they set up a meeting for you with a potential mentor? Do they have book recommendations? Do they have any tips, experiences, or suggestions that could help you? Even if you don't use their advice, they will appreciate feeling included in the process. No matter how much you prepare, your loved ones still might dash your dreams. Listen to their concerns, be respectful, and look for legitimate advice that can improve your plan. Take the rest with a grain of salt.

EXERCISE: Anticipate objections. Come up with a list of every possible objection or concern someone could have about your dream. Research and write a detailed response to each concern. Note: You can refer to chapter 5 for help with your research.

EXERCISE: Know your Circle of Trust. Who are the supporters and who are the haters? Identify three people you can trust to support your plan, ask helpful questions, and provide constructive criticism. Next, identify three people who are likely to make fun of your plan or discourage you. As you pursue your dream, be mindful of who you share your daily struggles with.

EXERCISE: Find your role models. Find three examples of people successfully doing what you want to do, or something similar. Study their success. What are five lessons you can learn from them and apply to your own vision? When explaining your dream to others, cite these three role models as examples for how you plan to be successful.

ROADBLOCK # 2:

FEAR OF FAILURE

"Inaction breeds doubt and fear. Action breeds confidence and courage. If you want to conquer fear, do not sit home and think about it. Go out and get busy."

—Dale Carnegie

Picture This: You really want to be a stand-up comedian. You buy tickets to comedy shows with extra cash, research open mics in your free time, and have a giant stack of favorite comedy albums and movies. You want to do a five-minute set at an open mic, but are paralyzed by the possibility of bombing. You decide to pass on this week's show and perform next month. Pretty soon, you're finding all kinds of excuses for not performing. This pattern of avoidance grows until you lose all confidence in your ability to make people laugh.

Root Causes: Humans are creatures of habit. Our brains evolved to seek out the familiar to keep us safe: a warm cave to protect from predators and the elements, recognizable foods, and a trusted, clean water source. Today, when we contemplate doing something new and risky, our old evolutionary programming kicks in. The idea of performing at an open mic is unfamiliar and therefore possibly dangerous, so we avoid it. We like to do activities we know will make us look smart, sexy, and capable. We want a guaranteed success. Because we know that life has no guarantees, we settle for inaction. After all, you can never fail if you never try.

How to Deal

Fear is a normal human emotion. As you contemplate something risky or new, recognize that fear is just one slice of your emotional pie. Curiosity, ambition, confidence, and excitement are all slices too. If you let fear dictate decisions, you'll never take a risk. Focus on your positive emotions to help you do something scary.

Also, shelve any expectations of greatness in your first attempts. Michelangelo didn't sculpt a masterpiece the first or fiftieth time he picked up the chisel. Amelia Earhart wasn't an expert pilot the first time she took flight. Steven Spielberg wasn't an Oscar-worthy filmmaker the first time he yelled "lights, camera, action!" Improvement is incremental and comes from risk-taking and a willingness to learn. All genius has humble origins. You can build confidence and conquer your fear with baby steps. An aspiring stand-up comedian could build confidence with the following small risks:

- Make a presentation at work to become more comfortable with public speaking.
- Play a team sport to get comfortable with riffing and making small talk with others.
- Attend a local comedy meet-up or club to connect with other amateur jokesters who can offer encouragement.
- Tell a joke to a friend in your Circle of Trust.
- Practice your comedy routine and timing in front of a small group of friends.
- Once you've wet your feet a bit and feel more confident, do the open mic and pack the audience with supportive friends and loved ones.

EXERCISE: This week, take a baby step to build confidence. Do something that scares you slightly: talk to someone new, ask someone out on a date, go out to lunch with coworkers, wear a new outfit that you think is too cool, volunteer to speak in public, or go to a new class at your gym.

EXERCISE: Have you ever really thought about what failure would look like? Write a paragraph describing a hypothetical failure. What would be the consequences? Be honest with yourself. If you fail, can you still find a way to feed, clothe, and shelter yourself? Couldn't you just try again? Don't exaggerate the effects of failure.

ROADBLOCK #3:
FEAR OF GIVING UP SECURITY

> "The trouble is, if you don't risk anything,
> you risk even more."
>
> —Erica Jong

Picture This: In Billy Joel's song "Piano Man" the bar patrons are delaying their dreams because they fear giving up security:

John, the bartender, who's sure he could be a movie star, if he could just get out of this place.

Davey, who's still in the Navy, and probably will be for life.

The waitress, who's practicing politics.

Many of us cling to security despite our true dreams. We tell ourselves: I'll chase my dreams someday, once I have more money, more time, more experience, once I settle down, once I get married, once two years have passed . . .

Root Cause: Chasing a dream might mean giving up safety, comfort, money, steady hours, a boss, a tested traditional path, or a routine. In short, pursuing a passion is a gamble and we don't want to roll the dice.

How to Deal

Dreams begin with small steps in the right direction, not huge leaps of faith. Pursuing a dream doesn't mean you have to quit your day job, move across the country, or do anything drastic. Our friends in Billy Joel's bar could move their lives forward with small steps.

> John, the bartender and aspiring actor, could join a local theater company that rehearses before work.
>
> Davey from the Navy could stop spending all his time in a bar and start working on a business plan during his furlough.
>
> The politician waitress could prepare a campaign for the local PTA instead of wasting all of her charm on drunks.

Chasing your dream doesn't get any easier as time passes. As life goes on, more financial and family responsibilities are heaped on your plate—bills, a mortgage, kids, and caring for aging parents. There is never going to be a perfect time for chasing your dream. Start small. Start now. Don't buy into the myth of security. Even if you have steady income and a job, you're never truly secure. Tragedy or challenges can strike at any time, no matter how much we prepare. Millionaires still have heart attacks, people who never break the law can still be the victims of crime, and the woman who avoids planes like the plague might wind up in a car crash. Security is an illusion. No one is promised tomorrow, there is only today. Start small. Start now.

EXERCISE: Take one small step towards your dream today.

ROADBLOCK #4:

YOUR INNER CRITIC

"Change your thoughts, change your world."

–Martha Beck

Picture This: Have you ever had any of these negative thoughts?

I never finish anything.

I love to make plans but I never follow through.

I'm too depressed (self-diagnosed), anxious, or nervous to do this.

I have too much emotional baggage.

I have a screwed up family.

I'm too lazy.

I'm not smart enough.

I'm not talented enough.

I'm not likeable.

I'm not good enough.

Root Causes: Negative thoughts can manifest when you feel like you are failing to meet the standards set by parents, peer groups, or yourself. We can trace some of these beliefs all the way back to childhood—your parents never hung up your artwork or came to your recitals, you beat yourself up for coming in third in the science fair, or you got picked last for dodge ball. Without enough reassurance, praise, or inclusion, we will start to believe that something is wrong with us. When faced with new risks or challenges, we dwell on our old doubts and fears rather than taking action. As time passes, inaction and stagnancy become a way of life.

Over-generalization and blanket statements are also the cause of negative self-beliefs. You do poorly in one math class and believe you are stupid. You get booted from the lunch table and conclude that you're a loser. Your voice cracks several times in choir and you label yourself a talentless hack. Isolated incidents become sweeping conclusions and soon, we have destroyed our self-esteem.

How to Deal

To overcome negative beliefs you need to:

1. Identify the source of your self-doubt. Answer:

- When did you first think or feel like this?
- Who or what triggered this negative belief?
- Why did it make you feel so bad?
- Why do you continue to hold this negative belief?
- How do you reinforce this belief through your actions?

2. Stop relying on others for validation. Spend less time with the people who bring you down. Life's too short to keep bad friends. Allowing another person to define whether you are good-looking, intelligent, talented, funny, or useful, gives that person far too much power. Ignore those who make fun of you. Walk away if someone says bad things about you. Don't give anyone the power to break you down.

3. Create confidence with your actions. Take action to feel good. Keep your promises. Do something nice for someone else. Volunteer. If going for a run makes you feel happy, go for a run. Or, make a change you can be proud of: "I'm never late, I always arrive ten minutes early." You're in charge of your life, so act like it.

4. Seek out aids to compliment your skill sets. Do what you are good at and leave the rest to others. You can always find partners or use technology to make up for any skills you lack. Do you have big ideas, but a problem with follow-through? Then make it a priority to find a partner with a Type A

personality. Bad at grammar? Use spell-check before you send out documents or e-mails. Don't use your negative beliefs as an excuse. Accept your weaknesses and plan accordingly.

EXERCISE: Come up with three concrete actions you can do today to improve your self-image. For example, if your negative belief is "I never stick to deadlines," put down this book and go do one task on your to-do list. Pick something easy: get your laundry done, write the first paragraph of your business plan, or write an e-mail you've been putting off.

ROADBLOCK # 5:

BELIEVING YOUR DREAM IS SILLY, SELFISH, OR FRIVOLOUS

"Laughter is the world's most important export."

—Walt Disney

Picture This: How can you possibly pursue your passion for comic books, aliens, and video games when you should be trying to cure a disease? How can you even think of becoming a playwright when there are starving children in the world? How will anyone ever take you seriously if you work as an artisan ice-cream vendor, write a teen romance novel, or open a vintage clothing store?

Root Causes: Chasing a dream that is enjoyable can lead to feelings of guilt. Society has taught us that work should be difficult and address serious causes. Who are you to have fun on the job while everyone else toils away? Traditional career paths are lauded above so-called fun careers. Most people agree that being a doctor is serious and important work, but are less supportive of unconventional dreams like being a comic book illustrator, teen romance novelist, or playwright. We only applaud the people in these untraditional careers once they've had a big success: a comic book becomes the plot of a movie, the novelist's romance flies off the shelves, or a director debuts on Broadway. Before then, you're a nobody—and that thought can be scary.

How to Deal

If you feel guilty about pursuing a fun career, think about incorporating activism into your life. There is no rule that a person can't have a cool job and help others too. You can be a cartoonist who also volunteers at a medical clinic, a comedian who performs for the troops, or restaurateur who donates extra food to the hungry. You've got plenty of successful role models: think about actor George Clooney visiting the Sudan, the Bill & Melinda Gates Foundation, or fiction writer Dave Eggers's 826 Valencia Foundation that helps teach literacy to school kids.

Get off the guilt-trip. Passion, in any career, has a positive impact on the world.

The *Star Wars* podcast you produce could make a lonely teenager feel like part of a larger community.

The song you write could play at someone's wedding or inspire a young person to be a musician.

Your artisan ice-cream shop could be the place where two lifelong friends meet once a week to catch up.

Ignoring your true dream in favor of something more serious will lead to regret. We can't change who we are or what we love. Don't deny your nature.

EXERCISE: Write a paragraph about something silly that has positively impacted your life.

ROADBLOCK # 6:

THINKING YOUR DREAM IS UNORIGINAL

"If you simply try to tell the truth (without caring twopence how often it has been told before) you will, nine times out of ten, become original without ever having noticed it."

—C. S. Lewis

Picture This: Have you ever thought:

My idea, product, or service already exists. Why should I even bother?

I wrote something, drew something, or created something I thought was original and a few days later, I realized it resembles someone else's work!

How can I stand out? I'm not special.

So-and-so is my idol and I've studied everything they've done. I just feel like a copycat.

I invented something that is basically a knockoff of someone else's idea. It's slightly different but nothing to be proud of.

Root Cause: We want to be special and significant. We want to change the world and be remembered for our individuality. So, we rip up any work that bears resemblance to another, abandoning our infant dream before it had a chance to grow and take on its own life. Worrying about originality is a sign you are spending too much time comparing yourself to other people. In truth, there is nothing new under the sun. Humans modify, borrow, and swap ideas all the time to make new products, art, and business models.

How to Deal

It's okay to be similar to someone else. There's Coke and Pepsi, McDonald's and Burger King, the bass line in "Ice Ice Baby" and the bass line in "Under Pressure." Entire brands and careers are created around subtle differences. Progress is all about building on existing ideas. Successful people stand on the shoulders of those who came before them. Roman philosophers relied on the Greeks, Galileo relied on Copernicus, Newton relied on Galileo, Einstein relied on Newton, Hawking relied on Einstein, and so forth. Einstein said, "To the Master's honor all must turn, each in its track, without a sound, forever tracing Newton's ground." Newton felt this way too: "If I have seen further it is by standing on the shoulders of giants."

There's only one you. The way you approach a problem, come up with a solution, or present your ideas is going to be different from everyone else on the planet, because you are a unique individual. Your originality will always show in your work.

EXERCISE: Celebrate your difference. Write down five experiences or traits that make you one of a kind.

EXERCISE: Read something new and strange this week. Sometimes we feel like a copycat because all of our ideas are coming from one source. Shake it up and expose yourself to the unfamiliar. Don't just stick to the required reading list.

EXERCISE: Go it alone. This week, take on a small task you've never done before, without looking up directions or advice. For example, write a one-page story, make up a recipe and cook dinner, or try your hand at making an origami swan. The point of this exercise is to get comfortable relying on your intuition to guide your choices, not someone else's instructions.

ROADBLOCK #7:
HERO WORSHIP

> "We shouldn't be looking for heroes,
> we should be looking for good ideas."
>
> —Noam Chomsky

Picture This: You idolize the established heroes of your field, whose stature and accomplishments you could never hope to live up to. You find a person doing something you want to do, learn more about that person's career, and then become obsessed with how talented, smart, and successful they seem. Pretty soon, you're spending more time researching someone else's work than doing your own.

Root Causes: We are a culture obsessed with heroes. We love thrilling tales of individual triumph, underdogs beating the odds, and everyday men and women rising up from their modest origins to do extraordinary things. We want to emulate our heroes, so we study them, eagerly lapping up every detail of their lives. What begins as honest admiration can descend into procrastination, unhealthy comparison, and unrealistic expectations. Unchecked hero worship will delay your own development.

How to Deal

Sometimes the less we know, the easier it is to begin. Too much hero worship can intimidate you. You only need to learn enough from heroes to get started on your own dream. It's okay to spend time picking up success strategies, do's and don'ts, and inspiration, but don't waste your time on extraneous, inapplicable details. There's no need to know your hero's favorite color T-shirt, where they get their hair cut, or their current relationship status.

Don't let hero worship make you feel inadequate. We only see the best of our heroes, not what goes on behind the curtain. Shakespeare threw things in the trash, Van Gogh made errant brush strokes, and even Slash couldn't play a C chord when he first picked up a guitar. Take your hero off the pedestal. They are just people like you. They put their pants on one leg at a time, same as everybody else.

EXERCISE: Pick one trait you admire most about your hero. How can you emulate that trait in your own life and actions? Describe three ways.

ROADBLOCK #8:

PARALYSIS BY ANALYSIS

> "The maxim 'Nothing but perfection' may be spelled 'Paralysis'"
>
> —Winston Churchill

Picture This: Do you over-think decisions to the point of inaction?

You try to imagine every possible outcome that could occur if you accept a job. While you spend a week making dozens of pros and cons lists, the company offers the job to someone else.

You spend so much time deciding whether or not to sign up for a street fair that you miss the application deadline.

You're making a bunch of to-do lists, but you aren't doing anything.

Root Causes: There is comfort in logic. It is reassuring to believe you can think your way through any problem, or always choose correctly with enough analysis. Over-analyzers struggle with following their gut instincts and believe logic is the key to all problem solving. Too much analysis can also be a mechanism for avoiding risks. After all, it's less risky to think than act.

How to Deal

It's healthy and smart to be well-informed about your career choices, but only up to a certain point. You have a problem when your endless quest for excessive knowledge impedes your progress and decision-making ability. To avoid paralysis by analysis, set a time limit for decision-making, research, and brainstorming. Try to make the time limit proportional to the task at hand. Choosing what color business cards to order should take five minutes of contemplation. Deciding whether or not to take on a loan should require more time.

If you're missing deadlines or feeling paralyzed, you need to learn to trust your gut instinct when faced with a choice. *But can we really trust our gut?* Research suggests that we can and should. In his book, *The Other 90 Percent*, Neuroscientist Dr. Robert Cooper has shown that the enteric nervous system, located in your gut, actually functions as a second brain. The enteric nervous system is an elaborate set of neurochemicals and nerve cells that is able to learn, remember, and influence our perceptions and behaviors. Dr. Cooper argues that decisions based on our gut instinct can be just as reliable as those made with pure frontal lobe logic.

The key to overcoming paralysis is to realize that mistakes are always possible, regardless of how much analysis you do. Here's the good news: mistakes aren't the end of the world. You can learn from them and bounce back. Don't waste an inordinate amount of time obsessing over what-ifs. Life's formula is pretty simple: try something, make a mistake, learn, and improve.

EXERCISE: This week, make three quick decisions using your gut. Make the decisions small and the stakes low.

SUMMARY POINTS:

• Everyone has roadblocks. Don't feel alone or embarrassed by your hang-ups.

• Tracing the root causes of your hang-ups can help you dismantle and overcome them.

• Roadblocks can be taken apart brick-by-brick. Don't let yourself get stuck in dream-limbo, paralyzed by your doubt and fear. Take action.

• Keep a bookmark in this chapter. Roadblocks will crop up at many stages in your journey.

CHAPTER 5:
MAP-MAKING

Create a plan for achieving your dream.

"Proper planning prevents
poor performance."

—a favorite saying of Dennis Lynch
(Alexis's Grandfather)

Often, we can see our dream in the hazy distance but the path isn't clear. We don't know which route is quickest, what crossroads to expect, or the landmarks we must pass before reaching our final destination. To achieve your dream you need a roadmap. Creating a step-by-step plan will ground your dream in reality, shed light on the behind-the-scenes work you need to do, and help you establish a timeline for success. This plan will also illuminate the first steps you can take to begin your work. So let's:

1. Make Your Step-by-Step Plan
2. Look at 25 Sample Plans
3. Use Research Tools
4. Make Action Items for Step #1
5. Create a Business Plan . . . If Needed
6. Make a Public Commitment

What's Your Mountaintop?

Before creating your plan, you need a specific milestone to aim for. As a medical researcher, your goal could be to cure a disease. As a web developer, your goal could be to reach 1 million hits a month on your site. As a writer, your goal could be to make the *New York Times* Bestseller List. Once you know the end result you want, you can start researching the prerequisites.

EXERCISE: Get specific. What is your vision of success, what milestone do you want to reach?

MAKE YOUR STEP-BY-STEP PLAN

It can be helpful to think about your dream as a ladder. You put the work in, climb each rung, and eventually reach your mountaintop. Let's imagine your dream is to be a rock star playing to a sold-out arena. Before you book a gig at Madison Square Garden, you need to reach dozens of smaller milestones. Your step-by-step plan might look like this:

Today:	Bust out the guitar, tune it up, practice for a few hours, and try to write some lyrics.
1 week:	Finish writing your first song.
2 weeks:	Play an acoustic set at a coffee shop.
1 month:	Recruit all the members of your band.
2 months:	Band should be fully assembled, rehearsed, with five songs written and mastered.
3 months:	Band should have a great website, a social media presence, and a street team for promotion.
6 months:	Band should be gigging regularly at local clubs and bars.
1 year:	Create an EP or a demo to get attention.
2 years:	Go on a regional tour.
3 years:	Get a record deal and release a first album.
4 years:	Go on a national tour as an opening act for a big headliner.
5 years:	Release a second album and be the headliner on a tour.

EXERCISE: Make your own step-by-step plan, similar to the example above. Don't worry if you don't know all the specific steps; just make your best guess and we'll add more detail later.

LOOK AT 25 SAMPLE PLANS

On the next pages, we've created twenty-five example step-by-step plans for a variety of popular dreams to help you get started. **Disclaimer:** these are just examples; your individual path or experience may vary.

Fashion Designer

Identify and track your fashion inspirations on Pinterest or an actual pinboard.

Pick a type of fashion to focus on—women's, footwear, accessories, etc.

Create sketches.

Take a class or workshop in drawing and sketching to get better.

Purchase fabric.

Learn to sew online or in a class.

Buy a mannequin to work with.

Start making clothes for friends.

Get an internship or apprenticeship.

Consider fashion school.

Develop a business plan for selling your original work. (See below in this chapter.)

Develop a portfolio of your work.

Participate in local runway events.

Plan your own fashion show.

Find a local retailer to carry your fashion line.

Open your own retail or online store.

Comedian

Figure out what type of comedy you like and attend lots of shows.

Study the comedians you admire. Read their biographies. Take notes on their style and timing.

Write every day—keep a journal or blog of observations.

Formulate the observations into jokes.

Test the jokes on friends and family.

Try a few open mics. Tape your performance. Review the tape to help you improve.

After several open mics, try to get a regular five-minute spot at a comedy club or host a weekly local show.

Network with comedians passing through town to become an opening act for a bigger comedian.

Participate in showcases and comedy competitions.

Network and perform a lot to get an agent or manager who can book you regular gigs.

Try to get on TV or get something filmed for the Internet.

Consider writing comedy in other formats—books, screenplays, TV shows, or a podcast.

Headline your own tour.

Create your first half-hour special (usually this can happen once you've been in the industry for ten years).

Author

Create a book concept.

Set a goal for writing 1,000–2,000 words a day.

For fiction, write the entire book. For non-fiction, learn how to write a book proposal.

Edit and refine the proposal or manuscript, possibly with the help of a coach or mentor.

Network or look online at publishersmarketplace.com to find contact information for literary agents.

Write a query letter to literary agents who have represented similar books.

Sign with an agent you click with.

Refine your novel or proposal and have the agent submit it to publishers.

Negotiate an advance and royalties and sign a contract.

Finish the book.

Work with an editor.

Publish the book.

Promote and sell the book.

Write a proposal for book #2.

If you are unable to attract publishers, consider self-publishing. Do a short print run that fits your budget.

Veterinarian

Consider a pre-veterinary program in college.

Volunteer or intern at a local vet's office, a farm, or animal shelter.

Take required classes set by the American Veterinary Medical Association.

Enroll in an accredited veterinary school.

Take a licensing exam and any required state exams.

Start a private practice or join an established group practice, animal hospital, or shelter.

If starting your own practice, choose a location and type of practice.

Finance your practice. (See chapters 7 and 8.)

Lease or buy the space.

Obtain licenses or inspections.

Hire the staff.

Purchase equipment.

Market the practice to the community.

Restaurant Owner

Create your restaurant concept and pick a theme (casual, Italian, sushi).

Pick a location.

Choose a name.

Write a business plan. (See later in this chapter.)

Find financing through loans, investors, and friends and family. (More tips in chapters 7 and 8.)

Apply for licenses and permits.

Design the restaurant or hire an architect.

Create the menu or hire an executive chef.

Stock the restaurant. Make deals with suppliers.

Hire and train the staff.

Pass inspections.

Launch a marketing campaign.

Plan a soft opening.

Invite local press and media to write reviews.

Add specials to attract new and repeat customers.

Computer/Video Game Designer

Develop skills in hardware, programming, and graphics.

Study computer programming, computer engineering, software development, or computer animation and graphics.

Consider interning or becoming an apprentice for an established company.

Gain experience by adding levels to an existing game in your free time.

Consider developing your own simple game to gain experience and build a portfolio.

Show your sample game to a video game company representative at a career fair, expo, or networking event.

Use your professors as references and connections to employers.

Work as a video game tester.

After working as a tester, seek a promotion to the development team.

Or, skip the corporate route and start your own indie game development company. See http://bit.ly/fUFu72 for a resource list for starting your video game business.

Professional Athlete

Determine which sport you are the best at and most passionate about.

Develop a training regimen.

Practice every day. Learn everything you can about the game or sport.

Excel at the school level (if you're in school).

Consider working with a private coach or personal trainer.

Work with your coach to get recruited to play in college or at the semi-professional level.

Keep your grades up and earn a degree.

Showcase your talents in front of scouts.

Join a minor league team or seek out competitions.

Work your way up to the professional level.

Supplement income by seeking endorsement deals.

Work Abroad

Pick the place you want to travel to.

Apply for your passport and any other needed documents.

Obtain a work visa.

Apply for a job, internship, or work-study program abroad.

Create a travel budget.

Create a basic itinerary—things you want to do, where you will be and when.

Book your plane, bus, train, or boat ticket.

Plan your lodging and pack.

Take care of miscellaneous items. Who will watch your dog? Do you need to add an overseas option on your cell phone? Do you need to notify your credit card company?

Learn about the culture, language, people, and customs.

Actress/Actor

Study acting. Take classes or workshops.

Get involved with local theaters.

Try out for the lead in a bigger theater production.

Act as much as possible, in theater, commercials, etc.

Once you've honed your craft, get headshots and write a résumé.

Send out the headshots and résumé to agents and managers.

Prepare for auditions by learning monologues.

Consider expanding beyond theater. Audition for your first film or TV show.

Make auditions a regular habit.

Make connections in the industry to get more parts or start your own independent film projects to get more attention.

Lawyer

Maintain a high GPA in undergrad.

Take the LSAT.

Apply to law school.

Get an internship at a law firm while in school.

Find a mentor while in school.

Graduate and pass exams.

Pass the bar exam.

Decide what type of job you want—large firm, corporate, judge's clerk, research, paralegal, pro-bono, criminal defense, etc.

Use your law school and mentor connections to seek a job and apply.

Chef

Start working in kitchens and restaurants.

Cook for friends, get feedback, develop recipes.

Find a local chef-training program or class.

Work at a restaurant.

Consider culinary school.

Seek an apprenticeship with a professional chef.

Obtain a certification from the American Culinary Federation.

Work your way up—chop station, line chef, sous chef, head chef, executive chef, and eventually master chef.

If you would like to open your own restaurant, take business classes and write a business plan. (See later in this chapter.)

Inventor

Identify a problem to solve or simplify.

Research your idea. Is it new or is someone else doing it?

Build a prototype and patent it.

Write a business plan. (See later in this chapter.)

Identify your market and method of distribution.

Do a test run of your product with actual people to get feedback.

Sell the rights to the invention or decide to manufacture the product on your own.

Find start-up financing for manufacturing. (See chapters 7 and 8.)

Create a marketing campaign.

Create a distribution deal with a retailer.

Sell or license the product.

Farmer

Decide the type of farming you want to do.

Obtain the skills you need for this type of farming through a local class or workshop, or by volunteering on a local farm.

Research or scout out land to buy.

Determine how much land and equipment you need and how much it will cost.

Write a business plan for how to monetize the crop you are growing, or livestock you are raising. (See later in this chapter.)

Find local support: suppliers, mechanical assistance, co-ops, etc.

Find financing. (See chapters 7 and 8.)

Purchase the land.

Sow the seeds, do a rain dance.

Grow, maintain, and sell your crops.

Teacher

Major in education in undergrad.

Intern or volunteer to work with kids in the age range you want to work with. Coach a summer team of kids, give swimming lessons, work at a camp, run an after-school program.

Identify the subject you want to teach.

Obtain a master's degree if needed.

Work as a teacher's aid.

Identify the state and district where you want to work.

Research your district's specific requirements for teacher's education and certifications.

Pass the Praxis exam, any required tests, or certification programs. Or, obtain a certain number of hours of in-classroom experience.

Join a teacher's networking group like AAACE, AACTE, NCTE, or NSTA.

Send out cover letters and résumés to the school district you want to work in and start the interview process.

Nonprofit Founder

Identify a need or cause and write a mission statement.

Recruit an organization of volunteers, board members, and staff.

Write a nonprofit business plan and articles of incorporation. (See later in this chapter.)

Create a detailed plan for obtaining fiscal sponsorship and donations.

Form a corporation at the state level.

Obtain an Employer Identification Number from the federal government.

Apply for tax-exempt status from the federal government using form 1023.

Enact your business plan, elect officers, hold board meetings, and get to work fulfilling your mission.

Web Developer

Decide what kind of web developer you want to be—web engineer, graphic designer, web producer, or a webmaster.

Study or teach yourself coding languages: XHTML, CSS, and Javascript.

Study or teach yourself programs like Photoshop, Illustrator, Flash, Fireworks, FrontPage, Dreamweaver, and Wordpress.

Consider studying marketing, art, and typography.

Build your own website to get experience and advertise your work.

Ask a friend or family member if you can build them a website.

Do some gratis web development for a nonprofit to add more experience to your résumé.

Search for paid gigs on freelancer.com, craigslist.org, and indeed.com.

Attend job fairs and use your connections to find job leads. Or, target thirty to fifty companies to send your résumé to.

Blogger

Select a topic you will enjoy continually writing about.

Sign up for Wordpress.

Purchase a domain and web hosting.

Pick a custom theme and design your blog.

Begin blogging, focusing on quality and consistency.

Build your online web presence through social networking and forum participation.

Increase traffic with guest posts, search engine optimization, joining a blog network, commenting on other blogs, and linking to other blogs. Most importantly, keep blogging.

Sign up for an ad network to monetize your site, like Google Ads, Foodbuzz, or Blogher.

Make money through services like Amazon's Affiliate Program. (You earn a percentage of the purchases made through your site.)

Reach out to companies that might want to buy ads.

Consider searching for freelance blogging jobs on sites like about.com, problogger.net, or bloggingpro.com.

Store Owner

Create or choose the products you want to sell.

Identify your ideal customer.

Research the demand for your product(s).

Write a business plan. (See later in this chapter.)

Work with a real estate agent to find a location that is likely to attract customers and fits your budget and size requirements.

When choosing a location, consider the population size, purchasing power, number of competitors, and aggressiveness of the competitors.

Consider traffic flow, complementary nature of surrounding stores, parking availability, zoning regulations, and personality of the landlord.

Decorate the store and hire contractors for plumbing, electricity, cooling/heating, etc.

Hire your staff. You may need a bookkeeper, sales associates, cashiers, and a marketing person.

Strike a deal with vendors to supply your products.

Plan a marketing campaign for your opening day.

Track which products sell well and which marketing campaigns are most successful. Read more: http://bit.ly/UxBV3P

Publicist

Study communications, journalism, English, or marketing in school.

Develop your writing and verbal communication skills.

Intern for a public relations firm or media company.

Work for your local or school newspaper.

Assemble a portfolio of press releases and articles you create during school and internships.

Search for entry-level jobs on journalismjobs.com and prsa.org

Polish and submit your résumé and cover letter to obtain job interviews.

Start as an assistant or junior public relations officer and work your way up.

Consider joining the Public Relations Society of America or the National Council for Marketing & Public Relations.

Architect

To become a licensed architect, earn a degree from an institution that is accredited by the National Architectural Accrediting Board.

During school, obtain an internship. Consider the NCARB Intern Development Program.

Pass the ARE test—Architect Registration Examination.

Create a clean, concise online portfolio.

Be creative in your job search. Get involved in an architecture blog, a forum discussion, a regional journal like ARCADE, or volunteer your services for a nonprofit to get a foot in the door.

Target a firm you admire. Attend their lectures, community events, or arrange to bump into them where they get coffee every day. Have a business card and résumé to hand out.

Journalist

Consider attending an accredited journalism school.

Choose a type of journalism to pursue—newspaper, magazine, photo, television, or online.

Complete several internships while in school.

Write articles, editorials, and blogs for as many local or school publications as you can.

Assemble a portfolio of your best clips to show potential employers.

Create a website with your résumé and links to clips.

Search for job openings on sites like journalismjobs.com, mediabistro.com, or your journalism school's online job board.

Let friends, family, clubs, and coworkers know that you are looking for a job.

Start with a local newspaper, magazine, or television station and work your way up.

Scientific Researcher

Plan on obtaining a Master's Degree and probably a Doctorate.

Take a broad approach in undergrad to find your niche—chemistry, biology, mathematics, physics, or computer science.

Obtain scholarships, grants, or fellowships to offset the expense of your education.

Go to graduate school. Participate in a post-doctoral program.

Assemble your curriculum vitae, including academic credentials and published works.

Choose between a career path in academia (the tenure pipeline), invention and industry, or government research.

Search for jobs online and upload your CV at sites like jobs.newscientist.com or jobs.phds.org.

Politician

Figure out your stance on the issues and consider becoming associated with a political party.

Practice public speaking, keep up with the news, and study history or law.

If you are still in school, run for class office.

Volunteer for multiple local political campaigns to gain experience.

Run for local offices—county or city commission, school board, or state legislature.

Ask friends, family, and volunteers to help run your campaign and fundraise.

If required, submit a petition with enough signatures to get your name on the ballot.

Schmooze with people who can help you get into office.

Campaign door-to-door, make calls, speak in public locations, talk with local constituents.

Publicize with lawn signs, bumper stickers, billboards, radio spots, interviews in the media, and paid advertisements.

After your term in local office, consider running for higher-level state positions and eventually, national-level office.

Doctor

Do well in a variety of science classes in all years of high school.

Volunteer at a local hospital.

Consider a college with a medical school as part of the university.

Choose a major you love but take the courses necessary for med-school (biology, chemistry, biochemistry, calculus, and labs.)

Maintain a 3.5 GPA or higher.

Pass the MCATs.

Apply to med-school and do well at your interviews.

Learn excellent time-management skills to cope with school.

Pass all three parts of the USMLE exam.

Choose a specialty in the fourth year of med-school.

Complete a 3–5 year residency.

Obtain a medical license and board certification.

Start a private practice, join a group, work at a hospital or clinic.

Professional Photographer

Read up on how to take good photographs. Become familiar with camera operations and technical terminology.

Practice taking photos locally, of friends, family, nearby parks, etc.

Take a photography class.

Take photos for your college newspaper or submit to a local news website.

Intern or work as an assistant for an established photographer or for a portrait studio.

Work for friends and family—weddings, graduations, etc.

Make a website with your photos and assemble a portfolio.

Join a photography organization like the American Society of Media Photographers.

Search for job listings and gigs and apply.

Connect with magazines or websites that are hiring.

Consider starting your own business as most of your work will be freelance.

Submit work to stock photo websites.

Plan a gallery event or sell prints.

USE RESEARCH TOOLS

If you don't know some of the steps in your plan, don't panic! We'll show you how to research the steps of your dream online. Let's imagine your dream is to become a museum curator . . .

- Start with the basics. Google "how to be a museum curator."
- Sites like ehow.com, wikihow.com, and howstuffworks.com provide general information: what degree or training is needed, tips on breaking into an industry, and the number of years the average person might spend in an entry-level position. *Be sure to fact-check everything you find.*
- Use indeed.com, simplyhired.com, monster.com, or the hiring section of your local museum's website to find out what skills, education, and experience is required for museum curators. What are employers looking for?
- Search online for interviews and videos featuring successful curators to pick up some tips for your plan.
- Search for museum curators who have blogs. Read their articles and take some time to look through the archives and comments.
- Search for online forums related to your dream like artcurators.org forums. Posters in a forum sometimes provide advice to up-and-comers.
- Go to meetup.com and look for a group relating to museum curators, history buffs, art historians, or job-hunters.
- Look up your town's historical society or museum. Read employee biographies, blogs, or news.
- Look at a local college or university website. Search the art, archeology, American studies, and history departments. Read every professor biography and see if anyone has worked in a museum, worked as a curator, or researched a topic you're interested in. E-mail this person to set up a meeting and ask them about their career.
- Google "trade magazine for museum curator." Visit any trade magazine sites and read articles that interest you. Study any job listings these magazine sites post—what qualifications are they looking for?

- Search for a specific topic you love, like "Civil War era clothing exhibits." Is there a curator who specializes in this area? Read more about how this person got started in the industry. Or, send them an e-mail with a few questions.
- Search for podcasts about museums or podcasts hosted by curators. Big museums or university departments usually have their own iTunesU channel. For example, the Smithsonian Institute has a podcast entitled "Curator's Introduction."
- Search online for biographies, autobiographies, films, TV shows, or documentaries to learn more about museums. Try documentaryheaven.com to watch thousands of films for free. Use amazon.com's related books features to find reading material about your dream.
- You can also look up a local career counselor to contact. If you are in school, you have free access to counselors who would love to help you. If you aren't currently in school, you can set up an appointment with a career coach for a small fee.

EXERCISE: Revise your step-by-step plan from the beginning of this chapter. Use the research methods above to fill in any missing steps or crucial details.

Warning: Avoid Research Overload. Learning the overall steps to achieving your dream shouldn't take more than a couple days. For now, don't go into excessive detail. Your goal is to identify the major milestones in your journey. Research is an ongoing process. You can do the nitty-gritty investigation about step #20 once you reach step #19.

MAKE ACTION ITEMS FOR STEP #1

Now that you have your step-by-step plan, it's time to make action items for step #1. If your first step is to get a gig for your band, your action item list might look like this:

Action Item #1:   Choose a target club, festival, coffee shop, or showcase that regularly books local bands of your caliber and style.

Action Item #2:   Research and create a list of similar venues within driving distance, in case your first target doesn't work out.

Action Item #3:   Use the Internet to find the promoter or talent booker's contact information.

Action Item #4:   Contact the talent booker with your pitch. Make the call, send the e-mail, go to the club, or send your demo package. Do this for multiple venues.

Action Item #5:   Offer to sell tickets to the show and do free promotion.

Action Item #6:   Follow up multiple times with the promoter to get an answer.

EXERCISE: Create a list of action items for step #1 of your plan. Do any additional research needed and be sure to attach a deadline to each action item. Once you get the gig and are ready for step #2, make a new list of action items.

CREATE A BUSINESS PLAN . . . IF NEEDED

If your dream involves being self-employed, you need to make a business plan in addition to your step-by-step plan. A business plan is a document that lays out your mission, goals, and how you will make money with your idea.

Who Needs a Business Plan?

Anyone selling a product or service

Entrepreneurs

Freelancers

Aspiring small-business owners

Inventors

If you plan to ask anyone else to fund your ideas

If you plan on seeking a partner

If you will be hiring employees

If you want to open a bank account for your organization

Nonprofit organizations need a business plan, as well as Articles of Incorporation and 501(c)3 status from the IRS

The best way to learn the language and structure of business plans is to look at real-life examples. For hundreds of examples of business plans go to sba.gov, bplans.com, and entrepreneur.com. They're great resources. We've come up with a list of elements most business plans should include, but be sure to research the specific requirements of your industry.

Elements of a Business Plan

Cover page: Business name and contact info.

Table of contents: Lists all the sections of the plan and page numbers.

Executive summary: One-page overview that summarizes the whole report.

Business description: How your business satisfies a need.

Business environment analysis: What is the outlook for the industry you are getting into? Why is it a good time to start this type of business?

Industry background: Your experience in the industry or other qualifications.

Competitor analysis: Prove that there is a market for this product or service by listing competitors who have had success in the field. Then, point out competitors' weaknesses and how you plan to be better than them.

Target market: Describe which demographic will want your product. For example, single mothers living in the city.

Marketing plan: Describe how you plan to reach your target audience. For example, Internet advertising, phone calls and e-mail, billboards, commercials, or magazine ads.

Management summary: Who is in charge, why are they qualified, and what is their vision for the business?

Operations plan: Describe the process of creating your product from start to finish. Where and how will you produce your product/service? How will you assure quality? What raw materials do you need? Who will be your suppliers?

Financial plan: Describe your plans to get funding, what expenses you are expecting, and how you will generate revenue over time (see chapters 7 and 8 for tips on budgeting and raising money for your dream).

Attachments and milestones: Include any other relevant information, achievements, or awards.

Note: If you need to write your business plan now, flip to chapter 10 for exercises to help you identify your target customer, set a price, and write a sales pitch. We've also included pointers on marketing, advertising, and publicity. For nonprofits, you can view an example Articles of Incorporation at: http://bit.ly/WPPWZg

MAKE A PUBLIC COMMITMENT

Once you have a dream and a detailed plan, make it public. Post it on Facebook and ask for input, blog about it, or tell a bunch of your friends. This may seem like bad advice at first. . . . What if you fail to meet your goal and everyone makes fun of you? Doesn't sharing your dream make you vulnerable? Yes. This is precisely the reason why you need to share. Public expectation is a powerful motivator. People will go to great lengths to avoid embarrassment or looking like a hypocrite. No one wants to be the person at the ten-year reunion who had big plans but never followed through.

The more people know about your dream, the better. Everyone loves to offer advice, share success strategies, and play matchmaker. Your best friend might just have an uncle who's looking to invest in projects like yours. Or, a gym buddy might know a web designer who could do your site for free. You never know who could be a key connection or give you a great tip.

Note: Don't go public with something that could put your day job in jeopardy. "See you later suckers, this is the year I start a business and move to Paris," might not be the best status update. Use your common sense.

If public commitment isn't your thing, at least tell your dream to your Circle of Trust. These allies can check in on your progress, support your early efforts, and provide encouragement and constructive criticism.

EXERCISE: Tell someone you trust about your dream and specific goals. See what advice and connections they have. If you feel encouraged, feel free to share your dream with more people.

Beginner's Luck

As you begin to enact your plan, don't be surprised if things start to click into place, you stumble upon something you need, or you experience a lucky encounter. The universe rewards those who commit to their goals. One of the most famous writings about the phenomenon of beginner's luck is from the Scottish mountaineer William Hutchison Murray. In his book, *The Scottish Himalayan Expedition,* he said the following after climbing the Himalayas:

"Until one is committed, there is hesitancy, the chance to draw back, always ineffectiveness. Concerning all acts of initiative (and creation) there is one elementary truth, the ignorance of which kills countless ideas and splendid plans: that the moment one definitely commits oneself, then Providence moves too. All sorts of things occur to help one that would never have otherwise occurred. A whole stream of events issues from the decision, raising in one's favor all manner of unforeseen incidents and meetings and material assistance . . . I have learned a deep respect for one of Goethe's couplets: 'Whatever you can do or dream you can, begin it. Boldness has genius, power, and magic in it!'"

SUMMARY POINTS

- Create a step-by-step plan with deadlines to demystify your dream.

- What's your mountaintop? Get specific so you know what to work towards.

- Do research to discover each milestone you need to reach.

- Create a list of Action Items for Step #1 and get started.

- If you want to work for yourself, you will need to write a business plan.

- As you chase your dream, don't stop learning and researching.

- Share your dream, make a public commitment, and don't be too surprised by beginner's luck.

CHAPTER 6:

FOOT TO PAVEMENT

Get busy with the right things
and find time for your dream.

"For disappearing acts, it's hard to beat what
happens to the eight hours supposedly left
after eight of sleep and eight of work."

—Doug Larson

Sometimes we feel like the busiest person in the world. Maybe you have a job with insane hours, a full course load and papers to write, children to take care of, or a loved one who needs assistance. Life is packed with time-consuming challenges. On our road trip, we met with dozens of successful people who found a way to balance life's responsibilities with their dream.

The eighty-hour-a-week lawyer who found time to write and sell a screenplay.
The mother of two adopted malnourished boys, who held down a job as an advertising rep while starting a health food company from scratch.
A full-time grad student who founded a social-lending business to help his community while keeping his grades up and working nights as a bouncer.

These people were not given a year off of work, a full-time nanny, or a personal assistant. Instead, they chose to juggle their dreams with the rest of life. You can choose to do the same. You don't have to go on leave or abandon family and friends to find the time for your dream. Dreams are built slowly, inch-by-inch, day-by-day, with each minute we put in and each small task we complete. Let's work on managing your schedule, ditching time-sucking vices, dropping unessential activities, and letting go of your addiction to busyness. We'll show you how to:

1. Make a Dream Calendar
2. Mind the Gaps in Your Schedule
3. Utilize the Fifteen-Minute Phenomenon
4. Increase Productivity by Developing a Ritual
5. Stop Saying Yes to Human Vacuums

MAKE A DREAM CALENDAR

In order to keep track of the tasks you have to complete, print or buy a calendar and post it somewhere you will see every day. First, mark down any important deadlines in your step-by-step plan that you want to accomplish this month:

1	2	3	4	5	6	7
8	9	10	11	12	13	14 *Complete 1st original song*
15	16	17	18 *E-mail 3 potential band members*	19	20	21
22	23	24	25	26	27	28 *Perform one song at an open mic*
29	30	31				

Now, fill in your Action Items on a weekly basis. Refer back to your step-by-step plan for this. For example:

Monday	*Re-string my guitar, 1 pm* *Practice 45 minutes, 6 pm*
Tuesday	*Practice 45 minutes, 6 pm*
Wednesday	*Guitar lessons until 5 pm* *Solo practice 1 hour, 7 pm*
Thursday	*Write lyrics for my song after practice, 6 pm*
Friday	*Practice 35 minutes before work, 8 am*
Saturday	*Compose music for my lyrics, 2 pm*
Sunday	*Finish my first song and practice it for 2 hours, 3 pm*

Schedule each task like you would a critical appointment you can't afford to miss. Put an "X" through each goal as you accomplish it, or circle goals you failed to complete so you know to get them done first thing tomorrow.

It can be tempting to skip weekly action items when you get busy or tired at the end of the day. In the following pages, we'll show you how to create time and energy for your dream.

EXERCISE: Track your time for seventy-two hours. When you wake up tomorrow, carry this book with you and fill in the following chart. Write what you did each hour, for the next three days. Include as much detail as possible and be honest: eating, sleeping, laundry, work, commute, surfing the net, watching TV, talking or texting with friends, working out. Don't try to do anything differently— just give an accurate description of your schedule right now.

Time	Day 1 activities	Day 2 activities	Day 3 activities
5 a.m.			
6 a.m.			
7 a.m.			
8 a.m.			
9 a.m.			
10 a.m.			
11 a.m.			
12 p.m.			
1 p.m.			
2 p.m.			
3 p.m.			
4 p.m.			
5 p.m.			
6 p.m.			
7 p.m.			
8 p.m.			
9 p.m.			
10 p.m.			
11 p.m.			
12 a.m.			
1 a.m.			
2 a.m.			
3 a.m.			
4 a.m.			

EXERCISE: Analyze your schedule by answering the following questions:

1. What activities take up the bulk of your time, besides sleep?
2. How do you feel about these time-consuming tasks?
3. Which activities increased stress?
4. Are you surprised by anything in your schedule?
5. In your opinion, what was a waste of time in the past three days?
6. What activities made you feel proud or good about yourself?
7. Could you do any activities more efficiently? How?
8. Was there any time you could have worked on your dream instead of doing something else?

MIND THE GAPS IN YOUR SCHEDULE

Rather than trying to clear out huge swaths of time for dream work, start with repurposing small gaps: fifteen minutes during lunch, forty minutes when you wake up, an hour on Saturday morning. Eventually, the small increments of time will add up and soon, you'll be making serious progress towards your big goal. Here are some possible gaps of time that could be used to work on your dream:

Wake up an hour earlier

Your lunch break

During a commute, while sitting on the bus, subway, or train

Waiting at the doctor's office or in line

An hour before dinner

The weekend

Any time that "disappears"—you can't look back and remember exactly what you did

Right before bed

Evenings after dinner

Waiting to meet your always-late friend

Instead of watching TV, checking e-mail, surfing the Internet, or texting

Look for gaps of time when you're most energetic and productive. As a night owl, working before bedtime will yield better results than waking up at 5 a.m. Don't strain against your natural tendencies.

EXERCISE: Identify three gaps in your schedule where you could work on your dream. Tomorrow, work on your dream during all three gaps.

UTILIZE THE FIFTEEN-MINUTE PHENOMENON

Even if you find gaps of time, you still might not feel like doing work. Sometimes, you just want to zone out to the TV, snack in hand. When you're tired, cranky, or unmotivated, put the Fifteen-Minute Phenomenon into practice. Tell yourself you only have to work for fifteen minutes. Think about your dream like exercise. Some days, the thought of going for a forty-five-minute run seems like torture. But, if you tell yourself you only have to go for a fifteen-minute jog around the block, it's easier to lace up your shoes, hit the road, and get moving. Sometimes the biggest obstacle is choosing to start. The first few minutes of exercise might feel unpleasant, but after a warm up you hit a groove, and suddenly running for forty-five minutes doesn't seem so bad. The same is true for working on your dream. The first fifteen minutes of work are probably the most painful, but after that, you feel ready to tackle more. Here are a few things you could accomplish in fifteen minutes:

Respond to five e-mails
Edit one page of a document
Write 500 words of your book
Write a short poem
Practice scales on an instrument
Sing or dance to three songs
Paint, draw, or sculpt

Make an important phone call

Brainstorm fifteen advertising ideas

Update social media

Write a brief blog post

Sketch an idea

Check your finances for the month

Search for a venue for an event you're planning

Edit a section of film

Take several photographs

Write a part of your rough draft

Work on your business plan

Practice your pitch to an investor

Send out three donation requests

The Fifteen-Minute Phenomenon will also help you stay consistent. Fifteen minutes of work is always doable, every day, no matter your mood or the circumstances.

EXERCISE: Stop everything and do work—for fifteen minutes!

INCREASE PRODUCTIVITY BY DEVELOPING A RITUAL

Many athletes have a set of idiosyncrasies they perform before each play, like the pitcher who rolls up his sleeves, grabs some dirt, and then dusts off his cleats before every throw. These maneuvers are habits that let the athlete know it is time to focus and get down to business. Your dream work should have its own ritual as well—a way to let yourself know it's time to concentrate. Your ritual could be lighting a candle, brewing a hot pot of peppermint tea, and holing up in the guest bedroom of your house. Maybe it could be heading out to the garage, cranking up the '80s hair metal, and strapping on your tool belt. Or perhaps you hit up the local coffee shop, get an espresso buzz, and start churning out code on your laptop.

EXERCISE: Answer the following questions to help define your work ritual:

1. What signals let you know that it's time to work?
2. What could you do to make your work more enjoyable? (Candles, temperature, clothing choice, or background noise)
3. What could you do to make your work time more productive? (Block the Internet, don't allow interruptions, leave your cell phone in another room)
4. Does music help or hinder you? Any specific kind?
5. Does being around other people help or hinder you?
6. What's your favorite time of day to do work?

Worst, First

You can also increase your productivity by starting the day with the most difficult task on your to-do list. Delaying a dreaded duty will only poison the day's otherwise enjoyable projects. Make a conscious choice to begin the day with a bang, not a fizzle. If you've been continually putting something off, drop everything and do it. The rest of your to-do list will seem easy by comparison.

EXERCISE: What task(s) have you been avoiding? Stop reading and go get it done.

THE PROBLEM WITH YES

It's easy to get sidetracked from your schedule. People are always asking for favors and we are eager to please, so we say yes to social engagements, errands, or projects we didn't really want to make time for. The end result? We wind up with a schedule that doesn't feel like our own and allows very little time for dream work. Here's how an addiction to yes can derail your dream:

A *colleague asks:* "Can you bake one of your delicious red-velvet cakes for the work party tomorrow? **The Consequence of Yes:** You agree to make a cake after work and cancel your plan to work on your sculpture.

A *relative asks:* "Would you mind picking up Tinsley again from her ballet practice? I was planning on it, but I really want to go out with some friends." **The Consequence of Yes:** You take a fifty-minute trip to pick up Tinsley, which leaves you with only twenty minutes of free time to work on your manuscript later that night.

A *friend asks:* "Do you want to go out to a karaoke party on Saturday night?" **The Consequence of Yes:** You agree to karaoke, and you're too beat to work on your website the next morning.

Often, we say yes because we don't want to offend or seem unwilling to go the extra mile. End your addiction to yes by presenting an alternative solution to the person asking for your time:

"I really don't have time to bake a cake, but I'll pick one up from the grocery store on my way to work tomorrow morning."

"I don't have time to pick up Tinsley today. Can you ask Marie, she lives closer?"

"I can't go out tonight. I have to work early in the morning. Rain check?"

You're time is precious. Don't give it up easily.

Signs of a Human Vacuum

A human vacuum is a person who sucks up excessive amounts of your time and energy. These are the people who always ask for favors without ever returning them, leave you feeling drained and tired, and pack unnecessary drama into your life. The signs of a human vacuum:

- Consistently interrupts you during work time
- Spends hours complaining about their problems yet never manages to ask about yours
- Asks big things of you with no payback

- Picks the most inconvenient time to ask for something—midnight on a work night, hours before a huge project is due, or the day of your birthday dinner
- Has a contagious negative attitude
- Draws you into doing activities you know you should skip: drinking too much, gossiping, blowing your paycheck, smoking, calling an old flame to yell at them
- Disappoints you by being unreachable when you need them most or flakes out on an agreement

These types of people monopolize your time and hold you back from dedicating yourself to your dream. If you are involved with a human vacuum, it's a two-way street. The human vacuum uses you, and you enable their bad behavior.

How to Deal with a Human Vacuum

If you have a friend, family member, or significant other who consistently makes you unhappy, crazed, or disappointed, it might be time to **seriously minimize your contact with them.**

Do your best to stop enabling the person's dependency on you. Stop acting like the other person's personal savior, assistant, chef, chauffeur, babysitter, psychologist, partner, police officer, or therapist, and they might stop treating you like one.

Talk it out. Have a calm discussion that clearly expresses how you want your relationship to change. You can't cure a drama addict with shouting.

Present an ultimatum. If necessary, you can present a toxic person with a choice: "Stop calling when you know I'm doing work, or I'll stop answering your calls all together. . . . I'm going to stop hanging out with you if you keep making me feel guilty about working late. . . . I'm not doing you any more favors until you do one for me."

Say goodbye. If someone crosses the line one too many times, cut them off. You can't focus on your goals when human vacuums are sapping your time and energy.

EXERCISE: Write a few paragraphs about the following: Are there any friends, significant others, or loved ones who monopolize your time or drain you emotionally? If you didn't have to spend so much time focusing on their problems, what could you do instead?

SUMMARY POINTS

- Many people balance dreams with work and family responsibilities. You can too, with creative time management.

- A physical calendar with monthly and weekly goals can serve as a motivator and checklist.

- Seek out gaps in your daily schedule where you can devote time to your dream.

- Employ the Fifteen-Minute Phenomenon to build consistency.

- Develop a ritual to let yourself know it's time to focus and work.

- Treat your time and energy with respect. Don't say yes to everything or enable time-sucking individuals.

- At first, you don't need to make a huge commitment to your dream, just make *some* commitment. Small chunks of time add up. Dreams are built inch by inch.

CHAPTER 7:
FEED THE PIG, PART 1

Reduce expenses to save
money for your dream.

"We best know our values when
we look at our check stubs."

—Gloria Steinem

All dreams require money. You need to get your finances in order before you can start a business, travel, buy supplies, or move to take on a new opportunity. Let's make a budget for Year 1 of chasing your dream and bolster your cash reserves by cutting back on personal expenses, like food and drink, lodging, transportation, shopping, and entertainment.

We'll also show you ways to beg, borrow, and barter to lessen dream expenses like new equipment, classes, or travel. The money you free up by limiting expenses can help partially fund your dream. In chapter 8, we'll look at ten ways to find outside financing for your dream.

Money is one of the most daunting obstacles we face when chasing a dream. A lack of funds can stop us dead in our tracks. Esther dreamed of running a Roaring '20s-themed bar. But how would she raise the money for a lease? How was Sam supposed to hire actors for his spaghetti western when he could barely afford a new camera? Alyssa had her heart set on becoming one of the nation's top neurosurgeons but feared taking on med-school debt she wouldn't be free of until middle age. What's a would-be doctor to do?

Sometimes, we lean on money like a crutch. We let vague fears of "not having enough money" stop us from going after what we want. However, the money you need is out there. Don't believe us? Walk down Main Street, go to any website, or flip through a telephone book to see hundreds of examples of people who found a way to fund their dreams. You can find the money you need for your dream by creating specific financial goals, spending and saving within a budget, and coming up with creative ways to raise funds.

The first question you need to ask yourself: *Exactly how much money do I need to start chasing my dream?*

DETAILS IN BUDGETING

Budgeting involves projecting and then tracking your expenses and income. Budgeting will help you determine how much money is needed to fund the initial stages of your dream. Let's start by focusing on Year 1. You need to imagine and research every single expense you expect to incur during this first year of pursuing your goals. This includes normal living expenses like:

Lodging/rent	Phone bill
Food	Medical prescriptions
Gasoline	Entertainment
Student loan	Utilities
Insurance	Bills

It also includes dream-related expenses such as:

Equipment	Tuition
Software	Class books
Research materials (books, subscriptions)	Travel
	Utilities or bills at your workspace
Membership fees	Licenses and permits
Leases	Insurance
Print materials	Technology (computer, hard drive, etc.)
Merchandise	
Advertising	Supplies (pens, paper, etc.)
New work clothing	Staff salaries
Gasoline/transportation (for work)	Legal counsel
Website domain	Accounting/tax help
Website hosting	Taxes owed
Rentals	

Just the Essentials

You probably won't need everything we just listed. What are the things you 100 percent, absolutely need to buy or pay for during Year 1 of chasing your dream? When projecting your expenses, only list the bare essentials. Do you need furniture for a home office right now? Do you even need a home office? Or can you get by just fine with a laptop and free Wi-Fi in coffee shops? Once you have a list of essential Year 1 expenses, do some research to find the approximate cost of each line item. You can find the average cost of most of the items on your budget through Internet sleuthing and asking people you trust.

Rule of Three

Whenever you research the price of a product or service, always examine three options to ensure that you get a fair price. Having three options will give you a good idea of what something is worth so you can avoid overspending. Some retailers will take advantage of your ignorance by overpricing items and hoping you won't do any comparison-shopping. Just like a hotel room can cost $70, $150, or $300 a night, dream-related products or services can also drastically vary in price. Use the Rule of Three to avoid being suckered, scammed, or otherwise sabotaged.

Online Resources for Researching Expenses

Lodging: Padmapper.com lets you quickly compare apartment prices using a Google map interface.

Gas: Gasbuddy.com tells you exact gas costs for a trip and updates gas prices in real-time to save you money. You could use this to budget a whole trip to the exact dollar.

Cell Phone Plan: Compare all carriers on whistleout.com/cellphones

Equipment and Technology: Pricewatch.com is a great site to compare the costs of laptops, hard drives, software, cameras, or just about any other electronic device you can think of. They also have a non-tech site that shows prices for clothing, home supplies, and outdoor gear.

Insurance: Try insurance.com to get an idea of auto and health insurance costs. The site sometimes requests personal information (name, address, etc.) before you get a quote.

Websites: Findmyhosting.com compares prices of web hosting and domain registration.

Entertainment: Get on Groupon and seatgeek.com to find cheap events and special deals.

Taxes: TurboTax makes it easy to figure out what you owe or what rebate to expect.

If you can't find prices online, ask three people you trust. This comes in handy for local services, like legal counsel, tax help, accounting services, or real estate. When in doubt, ask a neighbor, a parent, and a friend what they paid for these services.

EXERCISE: List all of the personal and dream expenses you expect during Year 1 of chasing your dream. Use the Rule of Three to find the cheapest option for each item.

CREATING YOUR BUDGET

Once you know your projected expenses for Year 1, it's time to create a budget. You can use Microsoft Excel or Google Docs (free) to make a spreadsheet and input your expenses for Year 1 of chasing your dream. Here is a sample budget:

Yearly Budget Example

Personal Expenses	Projected Cost	Expense Description
Lodging/Rent	$10,000	City apartment
Food	$1,800	Grocery
Gas (personal)	$2,400	
Student loan	$3,000	
Insurance	$1,680	Car and health
Phone bill	$720	
Prescriptions	$840	My meds
Entertainment	$2,000	Movies, nights out, etc.
Utilities	$1,200	Internet, electric, water
Car Payment	$2,400	
Toiletries and household	$600	
TOTALS:	$26,640	

Yearly Dream Expenses

Expenses Related to My Dream	Projected Cost	Expense Description
Equipment	$2,500	Camera, tripod, lights
Software	$250	Photoshop student version
Class on my dream	$1,500	Photography 101
Class books	$100	Guide to Photography
Website domain	$25	myportfolio.com
Website hosting	$80	10gb plan
Business cards	$25	Vista print
Travel to a conference	$200	Networking event
Gasoline to gigs	$400	Wedding shoots
Prints	$300	Hardcopy portfolio
TOTAL:	$5,380	

Yearly budgets are good for calculating your big financial goals. However, you may want to use a more precise monthly budget as well. Many expenses are incurred on a monthly basis—the rent is due once a month, the electric bill comes once a month, and the car payment is due once a month.

Monthly Budget Example

Monthly Expenses	Projected Expenses	Expense Description
Lodging/rent	$600	City apartment (w/ roommate)
Food	$150	Grocery
Gas (personal)	$200	Commute to work
Student Loan	$250	Monthly bill
Insurance	$140	Car and health
Phone Bill	$60	
Prescriptions	$70	My meds
Entertainment	$170	Movies, nights out, etc.
Utilities	$100	Internet, electric, water
Car Payment	$200	
Toiletries and house-hold	$50	
TOTAL:	$1,990	

The Magic Number: Year 1 Total Expenses

The magic number is your best projection of the total cost of chasing your dream during Year 1. You can find the magic number by adding up all of the personal and dream expenses in your yearly budget.

Once you have the magic number, we recommend adding at least 25 percent to it for increased security, inflation, and unexpected costs. Always overestimate your budgets. It's smart to expect high expenses and be pleasantly surprised when they aren't as bad as you thought. The 25 percent cushion should also give you enough time to get back on your feet if something goes wrong and you need time to figure out your next steps.

EXERCISE: Make your Year 1 budget and find your magic number—the total of all anticipated expenses. The next part of the chapter requires you to have your budget completed.

TRIM THE FAT

Right now, as you look at your magic number, you're probably thinking a four-letter word, followed by "I can't afford any of this!" Let's look at a few examples of trimming the fat:

You are launching a blog and want to hire a web designer. Alternative: Use a free website template like wordpress.org and teach yourself web-design basics using online tutorials and forums.

You want to be a filmmaker and need a camera. Alternative: Film your first project on your cell phone. Or, save money by renting a camera instead of buying a new one. Or, to start, buy a $200 video camera instead of a $2,000 top-end camera.

You want to be a fashion designer but need sewing classes. Alternative: Ask around to see if anyone will teach you to cross-stitch for free. Or, you could watch instructional sewing videos for free online.

You want to be a musician and need to buy recording equipment and software for your demo. Alternative: Use free software (like Audacity) or a laptop with a built-in microphone to record a demo. Or, you can borrow a mic from a friend or a school. It might not be high quality, but it will get you started. You can tell your fans it was an artistic choice, and you wanted the demo to sound "gritty" and "real."

You are living in the city so you can have your dream job. Rent costs $1,200 a month and is breaking the bank. Alternative: Throw up a divider in your tiny apartment and cram a roommate in your place to cut expenses in half.

EXERCISE: Go through your budget and examine each expense. Ask yourself:

- Do I absolutely, 100 percent need this expense to get to my dream?
- Can I change my plan to avoid or reduce this expense?
- Can I get the same result using a different product or service that costs less?

BEG, BORROW, AND BARTER

You can also trim expenses by asking for a donation, borrowing equipment, or exchanging favors. Think about what you need and brainstorm ways to beg, borrow, or barter for it.

- Do you know anyone who has what you need (a service, piece of equipment, or a workspace)?
- Would anyone trade something with you? Or temporarily loan you the item or equipment you need?
- Do you know someone who doesn't use their lawnmower/guitar/sewing machine/easel/fill-in-the-blank and would give it to you or sell it to you for a reduced price?
- Do you know anyone who performs a service you need (design, editing, or accounting) who would donate their time to help you in return for recognition or an I.O.U.?
- Does anyone owe you a favor? Could you exchange favors with anyone (clean Aunt Sally's attic every month in exchange for her legal counsel on setting up your business)?

People cannot help you until you ask. Just be polite and fair when asking someone to cut you a break.

E-mail/Phone Request Example

"Hi Uncle Mike, if it's at all possible, I would love your help working on my website this weekend for an hour or so. No worries if you're busy or unable to help. Can't wait to see you and Aunt Sally soon!"

- Use words like "if possible" and "no worries" to keep the tone light and give the other person an easy out if they can't or don't want to help.

- Always remember to pay back a favor when you can. Offer to help Uncle Mike clean his gutters or bring Aunt Sally her favorite dinner one night.

EXERCISE: Look at each expense on your budget. Identify one way you can beg, barter, or borrow for each item. For some expenses it may be impossible, but do your best.

NEEDS AND WANTS

A want is something you choose to pay and a need is something you have to pay. Each month, you can choose to pay for an unlimited data plan on your cell phone. You need to pay for food.

Cutting down on wants, or luxury spending, frees up cash that can be used for your dream. Eliminating all of the wants from your life is not realistic and can make you feel restricted or angry. **The point is not to get rid of all of the fun.** Instead, you should prioritize your wants. Which wants are most important to you? What could you cut back on?

Do you really need all these luxuries?

Sometimes you might really want the nicest, newest version of a product. Most times, however, you can get by just fine with a cheaper alternative. Ask yourself if you really need:

The largest cell phone plan	Trendy, brand-name clothes
A smart phone	Fancy hair and skin products
An expensive laptop	Brand-name household items
Cable TV	To go to the movies
A new car	To go to dinner
A huge DVD collection	To go on a costly vacation
To buy lots of MP3s and apps	To go to happy hour again

Just like you looked for alternatives to your dream expenses, you should look for alternatives to your wants that will still satisfy you. Some alternatives to the above "wants":

- Buy a cheap "pay-as-you-go" cell phone.
- Buy a friend's old laptop or a used one online.
- Use hulu.com for free streaming TV shows.
- Buy a used car or a bike.
- Use Redbox instead of buying DVDs or going to the movies.
- Use pandora.com or grooveshark.com to listen to free music.
- Only download free applications on your phone.
- Buy one or two trendy pieces of clothing a season; keep the rest of your wardrobe full of classics you can continually wear.
- Save money on hygiene products by using all-in-one soap like Dr. Bronner's Magic Soap, available at Target and health-food stores.
- Use natural cleaning products (lemons, white vinegar, baking soda) instead of expensive cleaning solutions.

- Have a fun night in with your friends. Activities like game night, renting a movie, or making dinner can be just as fun as going out.
- Go on a cheaper vacation, day trip, camping trip, or enjoy free activities in your city or town.

You don't have to eliminate everything fun and expensive, but thinking about what is most important (such as, I don't care about cable TV, but having an iPhone is really important to me) can help you decrease some of your expenses.

EXERCISE: Make a list of all your wants—the things you choose to pay for. Then, prioritize your list of wants from most important to least important. How can you adjust your spending based on this list?

PROBLEMS WITH SPENDING

If your spending isn't lining up with your wants and needs or there seems to be a hole in your pocket, ask yourself:

Are my spending habits influenced by peer pressure? How to take control:

Explain your financial situation and savings goals to friends and family. If people care about you and are aware of your goals, they should respect your new savings efforts and will be more open to cheaper activities or outings.

Suggest cheap or free activities: hiking, running, board games, matinees, coffees instead of brunch, lunch or happy hour instead of dinner and drinks.

Give an excuse if you really need to. Try saying things like "I just ate but I'd love to come hang out," or "I already did my spring clothes shopping, but I'll tag along to the mall."

Am I too whimsical or impulsive with my spending? How to take control:

Avoid people, places, or activities that trigger your compulsive spending. Avoid the outlets during the back-to-school shopping deals, for example.

Realize that spending binges provide a temporary happiness, much like alcohol, drugs, overeating, and gambling provide only a temporary high. You will probably feel let down after the quick jolt of joy evaporates.

Before you make an impulsive purchase stop and think: Do I really need this? Do I really want this? Why am I buying this? What will I use this for? What is more important: this luxury or my dream? With the money I'm about to spend, what else could I buy? (For example, this $5 coffee could be $5 worth of gas later and not purchasing this $20 dress could pay for half of my groceries tomorrow.)

Shopping can be an addiction. Seek professional help for out-of-control spending.

Do I set an unrealistic budget and blow through it? How to take control:

Don't set a reactionary budget. If you had a recent spending binge, don't create a draconian budget to assuage your guilt. Unrealistic budgets, just like unrealistic diets, are not sustainable.

Trimming down your expenses takes time. Don't expect to completely revamp your spending habits overnight or in one week. Give yourself time to get used to cutting back, and congratulate yourself for the steps you make along the way. As you become thriftier, set lower goals for spending.

Budget for fun. Allow yourself a set amount of cash each month or week for spontaneous purchases or activities you love. Sometimes, knowing you can spend money is enough to stop you from overdoing it.

Am I susceptible to trends? Do I buy things that are in fashion even if I don't need them? How to take control:

As tempting as it may be to own the latest product or gizmo, wait for Version 2.0, so you'll have a cheaper product without all the kinks.

Find alternate means of validation other than showing off your new toy.

Wait a while. Sometimes trends are over before they even begin. Trends that stick around longer than a few weeks are likely to be here for a while and might be worth the money. You'll be able to make a better decision about a purchase once the trend has cooled off slightly.

SAVING MONEY ON NEEDS

Although trimming luxuries seems like the most obvious way to get cash for your dream, you can also find ways to cut back on necessary expenses.

Lodging

For many graduating seniors or post-grads, it can be unpleasant to think about moving back home with your parents. But, if your parents are kind enough to offer free or cheap lodging, you have the potential to save a large sum of money for the initial stages of your dream. A good idea is to set a time limit on how long you will be at home, so you don't wear out your welcome.

If moving home is not an option, then search for cheap lodging. If you are searching for cheap rent:

- Get roommates to reduce housing costs. Splitting rent four ways means more money in your pocket.
- Rent a room from an individual instead of an apartment complex. Complexes can be inflexible about prices because of high demand, or amenities offered (a pool, a tennis court, a front desk). On the other hand, elderly people or fam-

ilies will often rent rooms or their basements to earn extra cash, and you have a chance to negotiate on a fair price.

- You can find free lodging by couchsurfing (a network of people who let travelers stay on their couch, couchsurfing.com) or WWOF'ing (World Wide Organic Farmers, wwoof.org, where you work on a farm in exchange for food and a place to stay).
- Downsize your space. A one-bedroom apartment is going to be cheaper than a townhouse.
- Subletting gives you a chance to haggle for savings. Also, you won't be locked into a long-term contract.
- If you are thinking about moving to a new area to seek out work, try to get a job before you sign a long-term lease. You need to have income before taking on debt.

Transportation

- If you live in an urban area, public transit can be cheaper than owning a car, especially when you factor in the price of maintenance, insurance, and gasoline.
- Walk, bike, or ride your skateboard whenever and wherever possible. A mile a day will save a tank of gas over the year.
- If you have a long commute, share rides with coworkers or neighbors going in the same direction.
- If you don't need a car every day, share it with a roommate or significant other to split costs.

Food and Drink

- Limit how often you buy food out. Preparing your own meals is much cheaper than paying for food on the go.
- Meat and dairy products are the most expensive items in the grocery store. For cheaper sources of protein, buy eggs, beans, and lentils. (You can find pre-cooked versions of beans and lentils, if you're short on time.)
- In-season fruits and vegetables will usually be the cheapest produce to buy.

- Invest in an insulated mug and brew your own coffee or tea. Keep your local coffee shop as a special treat, not a daily occurrence.
- A membership to a bulk or wholesale store (like BJ's or Costco) can cost money up front but can save you dough on items you use consistently—pasta, rice, canned beans, fruit, frozen vegetables, or meat.
- Some grocery stores have bulk bins, which offer pantry staples like beans, grains, seasonings, dried fruit, or nuts for a lower cost than their packaged counterparts. Bulk items have a lower unit price, which means the cost per ounce, pound, or gallon will be cheaper because you aren't paying for packaging or name brands.
- If you go out to a meal, split an entrée with a friend. Portion sizes in the U.S. are out of control and half of a meal is usually more than enough.
- Always search for bargain meals, happy hours, half-priced appetizers, or specials. Or, go to a BYOB restaurant with free or cheap corkage.

Clothing

- Never pay retail price for clothes, shoes, or accessories. Almost every item in a store will go on sale at some point.
- Don't buy something if it doesn't fit perfectly. If an item is too big, too small, or uncomfortable, you'll never wear it.
- Each season go through clothes, accessories, and shoes to donate (for a tax write-off) or sell items you don't want (try consignment shops or amazon.com)
- If you have friends with similar tastes or sizes, swap clothing instead of buying something new.
- Each new season, make a shopping list of what you actually need, not what is trendy. Buy what you need or will wear the most. A winter coat or a pair of jeans should take precedence over the latest fashion.
- Check thrift stores for unique or vintage pieces and cheap workout clothes.

EXERCISE: Go through your personal living expenses and brainstorm seven ways you could trim the fat and cut costs.

More Helpful Spending and Saving Tips

Make your money whim-proof. Put all of the money you don't need for monthly expenses into a savings account. Some savings accounts like ING.com take a few days to transfer to your checking account, which limits the risk of an ill-advised shopping spree. Your savings account should be virtually untouchable unless there is an emergency.

It's harder to spend cash than credit. If you are going to the mall, grocery store, or headed out for the night, leave your credit card at home and bring cash. Plan ahead, visit an ATM, and get the exact amount of cash you are comfortable spending. When the cash runs out, your spending is done and it is time to head home. It's much harder to watch dollar bills leave your wallet than it is to swipe a plastic card.

Don't make impulse purchases. Try to never pay for anything you didn't plan on. Stick to your shopping list.

Don't buy things just because they are cheap—or get sucked into sales because it's "such a great deal!" Spending money on things you wouldn't ordinarily buy is never a good deal.

For a more formal way of tracking expenses, we recommend mint.com.

WRITE DOWN YOUR EXPENSES

Keeping track of your spending with a weekly expense log can make you more conscientious with money, help change troubling spending habits, and allow you to set better financial goals.

This visual representation can assist you in your spending and savings decisions. For example, you might observe: "This week, I spent $77 on groceries, but half of my produce went bad. I can buy less next time around."

Weekly Expense Log Example

Week 1	$ Spent	Description
Tuesday	$325 $6	Rent due Magazines
Wednesday	$20	Prescription
Thursday	$3	Coffee
Friday	$77 $46	Grocery Party night
Saturday	$47	Gas
Sunday	$10	Lunch out
TOTAL:	$534	

To track your weekly and monthly spending, use an expense log similar to the one above or create your own. Every time you spend money, write down how much you spent and what you bought or paid for. Do this every morning. If you're bad about saving receipts, use your online banking log to fill out your spending log. At the end of each week, total up your expenses. You may be surprised to see exactly where all of your money is going.

The Benefits of Weekly Expense-Tracking

- Expense tracking lets you see past mistakes and helps cut back on spending the next week.
- The act of writing down numbers makes your money visible and can make you think twice about purchases. Sometimes knowing you have to write down "$7 for frozen yogurt" is enough to make you pocket your debit card.
- With an expense log, it's easier to do a cost versus benefit analysis to see if you truly like what you are spending money on. Was that $60 dinner really worth the money? Was that movie really worth $30 on tickets and popcorn?
- You will be more aware of expenses which leave you feeling cheated. If you are continually getting upset about paying $1,500 a month rent for your shoebox apartment, your expense log could push you to find a cheaper alternative.

Budgeting and getting your expenses under control will free up cash that can be repurposed to your dream. However, you may still require outside funding, which we will cover in the next chapter.

EXERCISE: Track your purchases for a week. Were you surprised by anything? Are there any areas where you want to cut down on spending?

EXERCISE: Challenge yourself to go five days without buying anything.

EXERCISE: Now that you have even more ideas for cutting back on needs and wants, take one more look at your Year 1 budget and see if you can cut, trim, or reduce any expenses.

SUMMARY POINTS

- Budgeting is an essential step in chasing your dream. You must get your finances in order before moving forward.

- When creating a budget, try to anticipate every expense you will incur for a year.

- Use the Rule of Three to get the best price.

- Beg, borrow, and barter to reduce your expenses.

- Search for do-it-yourself alternatives to expensive items on your budget.

- Use the techniques we suggested for reducing spending on needs or wants.

- Don't let peer pressure influence spending, don't be impulsive with purchases, don't set unrealistic budgets, and try not to fall for trends.

- Track your expenses to create accountability for spending and to make better decisions in the future.

CHAPTER 8

FEED THE PIG, PART 2

Raise the money for your dream.

"Money is only a tool. It will take you wherever you wish, but it will not replace you as the driver."

—Ayn Rand

Saving money will only get you so far. This chapter teaches you how to stuff your piggy bank with outside funding. For those of us who hate to fuss with financial details, this chapter may be a challenge. Power through it. Getting the funds you need is an essential step to making your dreams come true. Let's look at ten ways to raise funds. Feel free to skip around to the sections that are most applicable to your dream.

1. Weird, Wacky, and One-time Gigs
2. Fundraising Events
3. Crowdsourcing Websites
4. Sponsorships and In-kind Donations
5. Scholarships and Fellowships
6. Grants
7. Contests and Prizes
8. Investors
9. Take on a Loan
10. To Charge It or Not to Charge It?

Before we begin exploring fundraising techniques, let's reiterate an important point: In the initial stages of pursuing your passion, you should hold on to your day job and use any extra income to fund your dream. A day job is the most stable way to pay your living expenses while pocketing a bit of side cash. Most successful people had to keep their day jobs to pay the bills as they pursued their dreams in their off-hours. Madonna worked at Dunkin' Donuts before she became the Material Girl. Suze Orman, the financial guru, author, and TV personality, spent seven years working at a diner. Actor Jon Hamm was a teacher before hitting it big.

FUNDING METHOD #1:

WEIRD, WACKY, AND ONE-TIME GIGS

Here are a few non-traditional gigs you can do to bring in a little extra cash:

- Be a movie or TV extra. Check with your state's film office website for news on current productions (usually about $100 a day).
- Participate in a focus group. Register online at a site like advancedfocus.com to test a product or service (about $40–100).
- Be a mystery shopper. Business owners hire you to act like a shopper and then give feedback on your experience. Sign up on secretshopper.com (about $100 a month, or the equivalent in food and merchandise).
- Do fifty jobs on fiverr.com. Fivver is a website where people post small miscellaneous jobs that pay $5 each.
- Check freelancer.com. Get hired for short-term gigs in tech-support, web design, software, writing, design, data entry, sales, marketing, accounting, and legal services.
- Be a sign-spinner. Flip, jump, and dance with a poster board advertisement at a crowded intersection. Check out sites like gotchadirectionals.com/hiring to learn more ($10–20 an hour).
- Participate in a clinical trial. Search for hundreds of paid clinical trials at clinicaltrials.gov (payment varies).
- Participate in a paid study at your local college or university. Psychology, sociology, and philosophy departments often need to conduct studies on test subjects. Search your local school's website to find studies that need participants.
- Clean out people's garages, attics, closets, or sheds for a flat fee.
- Grow, brew, cook, or bake something to sell at a farmer's market, craft fair, or flea market.
- Buy and re-sell antiques, collectibles, or trading cards for a profit online or to a dealer.

Want a more stable way to earn extra cash? What about one of the following jobs: bartend, work at a department store, coach a team, tutor, babysit, clean houses, work at a restaurant, landscape and do yard work, work for a temp agency, get a sales job, work as a delivery person, work in construction or repairs, work in a grocery shop, gym, nursery, or hardware store, be an usher in a movie theater, work as a personal assistant, be a janitor, or be a barista at a coffee shop.

FUNDING METHOD #2:

FUNDRAISING EVENTS

Rake in some dollars for your dream by planning an event and asking for voluntary contributions in the form of money, supplies, or services. Whether you want to throw an informal shindig or a black-tie gala, an event is the perfect way to get lots of potential donors in one place and encourage the spirit of giving. Here's how to plan your fundraiser:

1. Pick a theme. It could be Luau, Fondue Night, a Studio 54 disco dance party, chili cookoff, or a golf tournament. Pick a theme that seems fun, appeals to a large crowd of donors, fits with the time of year, and most importantly, is profitable.

2. Reserve a venue. It could be your house, a friend's place, community room, a restaurant, game room, a bowling alley, a park, or a museum. Try to use your connections to reserve a free or cheap venue.

3. Pick a date and time that doesn't conflict with any other major holidays or events.

4. Create a budget and stick to it. You want to earn money from this event, not sink your resources into it.

5. Plan the food and entertainment. What will put your crowd in a generous mood? Music, bands, games, contests, dancing, karaoke, food, or specialty drinks?

6. Invite and promote. Remind people about the date, time, and location, in

multiple ways. Use posters, e-mail, social networks, phone calls, and mass texts to spread the word. To make the event even bigger, ask people to bring friends or contact the press if the event is open to the public.

7. Be clear about your cause. Suggest a donation amount and make sure people know exactly how their money will be used.

8. Provide multiple ways for people to give. Don't limit yourself to a single donation source. Charge at the door, sell tickets in advance, charge for food or drinks, have a tip jar, take checks, or hold a raffle or auction. You can also accept credit and debit cards on your iPhone, Android, or iPad by registering on squareup.com.

Fundraiser Event Tips

Target the big fish. Who are the people who can afford to give more? Make it a priority to invite them, treat them well, or get their input on the event. Also, make it family-friendly. You want as many people as possible to attend.

Hold raffles. In addition to the other entertainment at your event, raffles are good ways to draw a crowd and raise additional money. Possible raffle prizes include: a signed piece of memorabilia, tickets to a concert, or a coupon for a free massage at the local day spa. Reach out to local businesses to get the raffle item donated. Don't give your raffle items away for cheap. If you have a minimum amount of money you need to make, put a disclaimer on the item—"Must sell 500 tickets to raffle the Hawaiian Vacation." If you have a small-scale event, you could raffle something fun, low-cost, and creative like a home cooked three-course meal or a piece of art you made.

Have an auction. Auctions are another lucrative event addition. Common auction items include antiques, jewelry, designer or vintage clothing, furniture, or other collectibles. You will probably need an auctioneer or emcee to oversee the auction process. Again, try to get auction items donated so you don't have to spend money acquiring them.

FUNDING METHOD #3:
CROWDSOURCING WEBSITES

A crowdsourcing website lets you create a donation page to raise funds for film, music, art, charity, small businesses, gaming, theater projects, and more. Indiegogo.com and kickstarter.com are the most popular crowdsourcing sites. Most sites require an application, and once accepted, you create a page for your project with videos, pictures, information, donation levels, and rewards. Crowdsourcing websites provide a legitimate and easy way for friends, family, and strangers to donate to your project or cause.

These sites are for works already in progress: a rough cut of a movie, a half-finished video game, or a prototype of a product you want to sell. Don't apply until you have something to show. Be realistic with your funding goal. Some websites have time requirements (sixty days or less to fund) or all-or-nothing funding (if you don't meet your donation goal, you get nothing). Be sure you know any requirements and risks before investing time or energy into a crowd-sourcing campaign. Once you are accepted to a website, then the work begins to squeeze money out of anyone and everyone in your network. Here is a sample plan to spread the word about your funding campaign:

Day 1

Contact my alma mater's publicity department to see if they will write a story about my project. Contact Mom and Dad and ask them to forward my donation request to the people in their offices: Dave, Ursula, Shelia, Susan, Bill, Connell, and John. Share on personal Facebook and Twitter—every day.

Day 2

Write a press release to send to the local county newspaper. Send donation requests to Uncles Bob, Rick, and Gary. Ask them to forward the e-mail to anyone they know.

Day 3

Contact the rest of my extended family—Grandpa Dennis, Grandmas Sandy and Winoa, Kim, Karen, Cousins Laura, Becky, Caitlin, Meaghan, Bobby. Ask them to spread the word to their networks, forward our project page, and share on their social media.

Day 4

Contact my old friends from the soccer league. Contact the people from the church trip last summer. Ask the woman who makes the church newsletter to give it a short mention next week.

Day 5

Contact professors from college. Ask them to post my project page on their social media and forward to anyone who might be interested.

Day 6

Send out an e-mail to my neighborhood's listserv and post on our neighborhood blog. Send out an e-mail to all of my Facebook friends to see if they will post a message and link to my project page on their social media.

Day 7

Contact Joe, a potential investor and mentor, to see if he would donate or support the project.

Day 8

Contact Michael, a professor who has his own radio show, to see if I could come on the air.

Day 9

Contact Jared, my college advisor, and my coworkers and friends from my college jobs: Ed, Jake, Ryan, Chris, Dan, Kelli, Will, Wes, and Chelsea.

Day 10

Contact the representative of a corporate sponsor, who I met at a charity event, for a donation request.

Day 11

Talk to my sister Kelly about spreading the word to her friends at school and their parents. Reach out to my friends again (Kristen, Katie, Kunal, Lauri, Erin, Pat, Bailey) to ask them to forward my campaign to everyone in their address book.

Day 12

Contact five people from my former job to ask them to donate and help spread the word.

Day 13

Ask Chris, my friend who is popular on Twitter, if he can get me a retweet about my project page from a celebrity.

Day 14

Ask my friend Rachel in Charleston if she can get three buddies to donate $10 each. Contact people I've stayed close with from my three internships and ask them to share the link on their social media.

Day 15

Contact my friends in Philadelphia and Sacramento to ask if they can spread the word around town. Call in a favor that my friend Molly owes me and ask her to donate a small amount.

Day 16

Contact seven blogs and ask if I can write a guest post about my project. Reach out on Facebook again to acquaintances from college and high school that may be interested.

Day 17

Contact three teachers from high school. Contact former athletics coaches—Adam, Doug, Stan, Jeff, John, and Kevin.

Day 18

Send a personal e-mail to family friends I'm close with—the Lynchs, Trenners, Gibsons, Glenns, and Machcinskis.

Day 19

Begin contacting people associated with my project and ask them to spread the word in their town. Contact my extended family in Cincinnati.

Day 20

Write a blog for the *Huffington Post* Impact section.

Day 21

Post a video update about the fundraising campaign on my social networks. Attend an event where my friend's band is playing—ask to get on stage and announce my project.

Day 22

Send a press release to a local TV station. Connect with the creators of a podcast related to my dream to ask them to mention my project or have me on as a guest.

Day 23

Donate small amounts of money to three other projects in the hopes they will return the favor and spread the word.

Day 24

Follow up with everyone I have talked to so far to encourage them to increase their donation or donate a small amount if they haven't yet. Post on ten forums related to my dream, asking people to donate and spread the word.

Day 25

Reach out to everyone who has donated so far and ask each of them to tell five new people about the project. Create sidewalk art and hang up flyers all over town telling people there is one day left to reach my funding goal. Encourage people to give a small amount and help make my dream come true.

FUNDING METHOD #4:

SPONSORSHIPS AND IN-KIND DONATIONS

A sponsorship is when a company gives you money, free products, or services and in return, you advertise and promote their brand. To secure sponsors:

1. Determine the price of sponsorship. How much money are you asking for and what will the sponsor get in return? Consider offering tiered sponsorship levels, like Gold Level, Silver Level, and Bronze Level.

2. Here are a few ways you can promote your sponsor:

- Put their logo in a high-traffic location like your website, print materials, merchandise, a banner at your event, or on your car.
- Mention your sponsor on your social media sites.
- Give away a sponsor's promotional materials or products at events.
- Write product reviews about your sponsor online.
- Endorse a sponsor in a press release.
- Give your sponsor a booth at your event or allow their mascot to attend.
- Make an announcement about your sponsor at an event, on the radio, on TV, in a newspaper, magazine, or blog.
- Wear clothing with the company's logo on it when you are in public.

3. Target companies, organizations, or individuals that have a similar mission or audience.

4. Write your pitch to sponsors. Start by answering the following:

- Why should this business sponsor you? What are the benefits?
- How many people do you think you can reach? How will you do this?
- What audience are you reaching? Why is this good for the sponsor?
- Can your sponsor get positive publicity for supporting you or your cause?

Sponsorship Pitch Example

Hi Bob—

My name is Chip Hiden and I am the founder of the Chipapalooza Charity Concert for diabetes research. I went to school with your daughter Laura. I wanted to get in touch with you about our annual concert to see if Bob's Diner would become a sponsor of CCC this year. Hundreds of high-school kids attend the event every year and becoming a sponsor will create excellent exposure for the diner.

We started Chipapalooza when I was a senior at Reservoir High School in 2005. Around that time, I was diagnosed with diabetes and decided to throw a charity concert, donating all of the proceeds to the Juvenile Diabetes Research Foundation. Since that first concert, we have donated over $10,000 to the JDRF and had over 5,000 attendees. This year, Chipapalooza will be held at the minor league baseball stadium and will feature live music, an evening baseball game, and fireworks. In addition to including Bob's Diner on all of our print advertising, we could:

- Mention your support of the event during six of our scheduled radio interviews.

- Promote Bob's Diner on our Facebook, Twitter, blog, and YouTube pages.

- Offer you a table at the event to hand out marketing materials and distribute coupons to every attendee.

- Print the Bob's Diner logo on the back of the concert T-shirts.

- Hang a Bob's Diner banner on the stage.

There are many other possibilities and I would love to hear your ideas and suggestions. Thank you so much for your time and consideration. I look forward to hearing back from you. Feel free to write or call me.

FUNDING METHOD #5:

SCHOLARSHIPS AND FELLOWSHIPS

A scholarship is financial aid, given to a student to further their education. Scholarships can be given based on merit, GPA, geographic location, financial need, career or major focuses, race and ethnic heritage, gender, religion, sexual orientation, military and veteran status, disability, and family and medical history.

Scholarships

The search for scholarships can be overwhelming. To get started, search for something specific, like "scholarships for Hispanic women in Arkansas." Use scholarship databases like finaid.org/scholarships or the collegedata.com Scholarship Finder Widget. Talk to your guidance counselors for advice. If you are currently employed, see if your company offers financial aid for continuing education. If not, show your human resources department or boss how additional learning would positively impact the company's bottom line.

There are also scholarships to attend workshops, events, and conferences. The South by Southwest conference has a scholarship program for people "using technology or new media to do the most innovative work for good within their community."

Fellowships

Fellowships are merit-based monetary awards for academic work. Fellowships usually offer stipends to offset living expenses but they typically pay less than a full-time job. Aside from a stipend, other benefits of a fellowship may include student loan repayment, health care coverage, or free housing. Fellowships provide professional development and intensive training to help students conduct research or develop a community-based initiative. To find a fellowship, check out your school's website, visit the fellowship office, or start with this list of resources:

U.S. Education Department's Jacob K. Javits Fellowships Program

Guggenheim Fellowships for the Creative Arts

National Science Foundation Graduate Research Fellowship Program

Environmental Protection Agency's Science to Achieve Results (STAR) Fellowships for Graduate Environmental Study

Fulbright International Educational Exchange Program

Columbia University School of Arts and Science Fellowship Search

Cornell University Graduate School Fellowship Database

PPIA's Public Policy and International Affairs Fellowship Program

American Association for the Advancement of Science (congressional, diplomatic, and global policy fellowships)

Association for Schools of Public Health

Centers for Disease Control and Prevention

Environmental Protection Agency

The Greenlining Institute

Smithsonian Astrophysical Observatory

Smithsonian National Air and Space Museum

Smithsonian Tropical Research Center

U.S. Agency for International Development

U.S. Department of State

U.S. National Oceanic and Atmospheric Administration

Women's Research and Education Institute

The Woodrow Wilson National Fellowship Foundation

FUNDING METHOD #5:

GRANTS

Grants are funds given by one party (the government, a foundation, a trust, a corporation, a department) to a recipient. Grants can be for individuals, businesses, a nonprofit, or a school. Grants usually fund a specific cause: $1,000 for updating a nonprofit's website, $20,000 to implement a healthy eating habits program in local elementary schools, or $6,000 to attend a writing conference out of state.

You need to fill out an application to receive a grant—a lengthy and arduous process. For help filling out grant applications, pick up two books: Ellen Karsh and Arlen Sue Fox's *The Only Grant-Writing Book You'll Ever Need*, and Jane C. Geever's *The Foundation Center's Guide to Proposal Writing*. To begin searching for grants, start local, looking at grants in your town, school district, county, parish, region, and your state. Once you've exhausted any local possibilities, search for national grants online. Here are a few places to start:

The Foundation Center: The world's leading source of information on philanthropy, fundraising, and grant programs (foundationcenter.org)

GrantStation: For organizations seeking grants, some features on the site are free, others will cost money (grantstation.com)

Grants.gov: Announces federal grants and is helpful for nonprofits

The Grantmanship Center: tgci.com

Here are a few field-specific grant resources:

Art Grants

New York Foundation for the Arts: nyfa.org

National Endowment for the Arts: nea.gov/grants/apply

Pick up: *Grants for Artists* by Gigi Rosenberg

Education Grants for Students, Teachers, Classrooms, or Schools

NEA: neafoundation.org

Grants Alert: grantsalert.com

Bill & Melinda Gates Foundation: gatesfoundation.org

The Spencer Foundation: spencer.org

Pick up: *The Educator's Guide to Grants: Grant-Writing Tips and Techniques for Schools and Non-profits* by Dr. Linda Karges-Bone

Nonprofit Grants

Federal Grants: grants.gov/applicants/find_grant_opportunities.jsp

Fundsnet Services: fundsnetservices.com

Grant Gopher Database: grantgopher.com ($10 monthly fee)

Scientific Research Grants

U.S. Small Business Administration Scientific Research Grants: sba.gov/content/research-grants-small-businesses

enGrant Scientific: search.engrant.com

National Science Foundation: nsf.gov/funding

National Institutes of Health: grants.nih.gov/grants/guide

Humanities Research Grants

Harry Frank Guggenheim Foundation: hfg.org/rg/guidelines.htm

National Endowment for the Humanities: neh.gov/grants

American Council of Learned Societies: acls.org/grants

Pick up: *The Chronicle of Higher Education*, which usually reserves the last few pages to list grants and their deadlines

Business Grants

Grants for Women: grantsforwomen.org

Grants for Social Entrepreneurs: skollfoundation.org

Dosomething.org Grant Database: dosomething.org/grants/database

FUNDING METHOD #7:

CONTESTS AND PRIZES

In New Orleans, we spoke with Lavonzell Nicholson, who won $100,000 in the 504ward Business Plan Competition. Lavonzell used the prize money to launch playNOLA, a sports and social club designed to help young people meet, greet, and compete with others in the Big Easy. Could a contest fund your dream or provide some cash?

The Society of American Travel Writers distributes nearly $20,000 a year in prizes.

The Top Gun National Mock Trial Competition awards a $10,000 prize to a team of aspiring litigators.

The U.S.A. Songwriting Competition offers a $50,000 prize and radio play for original musicians.

The Scotch "Off the Roll" contest awards $6,500 in prizes to sculptors who make a piece of art out of Scotch tape.

The Grow St. Louis Contest gave $5,000 to Southwestern High School's Future Farmers of America chapter.

Amazon Movie Studios created a "pitch battle" where screenwriters faceoff online, present their movie premise, and users vote for their favorites. Amazon keeps tabs on the popular movie pitches, and offers some of the best a $10,000 development track deal and $200,000 if the movie gets made.

Bizplancompetitions.com is a comprehensive collection of competitive funding opportunities for start-ups.

Contestwatchers.com lists visual arts contests around the world. They also have scholarship and residency resources.

FUNDING METHOD #8:

INVESTORS

Investors are people who commit funds to your dream, with the expectation that their money will be paid back with additional interest, by a certain date. "Angel" investors are affluent individuals who contribute a large sum of money to launch your business in return for partial ownership.

Before seeking an investor, you should have already devoted time, energy, and funds into your business. You can demonstrate your commitment through a list of current clientele, schooling or training you've done, revenue you've generated, or something you've built on your own. Investors want numerical proof your idea can make money—do a trial run or a test market so you have data to present. Try to have samples and examples of your work: designs you have created, prototypes of your product, or an online portfolio. Be sure to have a detailed budget and financial plan that includes the specific amount of money you want to grow your business. Investors want to know that each dollar will be put to good use. Prove their funding will lead to growth and even more profit.

Start your search for investors by asking friends, family, friends of the family, teachers, professors, team members, old coworkers, old coaches, members of a club you belong to, or other business owners. Are any of them interested in investing? Or can they refer you to someone? Friends, family, and friends-of-friends, are the most common types of investors in the early stages of your business. If someone close to you decides to invest, make sure to agree on investment terms and create a contract together. Treat this investment the same as you would with an outsider. You don't want to sully a personal relationship over a future disagreement.

Spread your call for investors far and wide. Make it a point to speak and network at events, conferences, and meetings you attend. Try visiting your local Chamber of Commerce. Most of the people in the council had to raise start-up capital or get an investor at some point. Ask them how they did it. Or, search online for venture capitalists who make their living investing in new businesses. Be sure to double-check their credentials and speak with references.

You can also target investors that will benefit from your product or service. Could your invention help a big company save or make more money? Starbucks invested in SquareUp, the company that allows credit and debit payments to be accepted on mobile devices. Starbucks plans to use SquareUp's technology in 7,000 stores nationwide.

Once you've identified a potential investor, it's time to pitch your idea to them. You can begin with an introductory e-mail to gauge interest.

Investor Pitch Example

My name is Alex Treverson, I am a twenty-two-year-old graphic designer. Since graduating from State University, I've started my own graphic design business. Over the last year I have built a client base of twenty local businesses that place regular orders.

I am seeking funding for a printing press so I can better serve my clients' needs and reduce printing expenses, which I am currently outsourcing. Last year, my business brought in revenue of $11,254 and is growing at a rate of 122% per year.

The printing press would generate an extra $7,200 of income and would pay for itself within three months. I read that you supported Paul's Prints in Townnextdoor and I thought you might be interested in a similar investment opportunity. If you're interested in speaking, please give me a call.

If you get a bite, here are some questions to be prepared for:

- How much money do you need and why?
- What are the significant purchases you plan to make?
- How much revenue do you realistically expect to generate? What research do you have to support this?
- What unique need are you meeting? Or, what is unique about your business?
- Why are you qualified to do this?

- What are the risks of this business?
- Who are your competitors?
- What gives you an advantage?
- When will you break even?
- How will you obtain and retain customers?
- How will you keep customers happy and respond to complaints?
- Do you have any other partnerships?
- What is your plan for growth if your business becomes popular? How will you scale your business if demand increases?
- What is your exit strategy if the business fails or becomes unprofitable?

An investor's time is valuable so keep it short and sweet. If you can't explain your business, product, or service in a sentence, how is anyone else supposed to? Don't use big words if you don't know what they mean. Avoid corporate-speak, industry jargon, slang, or any other gimmicks. You're not going to get bonus points for trying to sound clever or slick.

It's also good practice to not include your salary in a business plan's budget. Let the investor know that the financial health of the business is your first priority and getting paid can wait. When presenting the budget, show them you have a grasp on reality with your revenue projections. Don't say you are going to grow from $10,000 in revenue to $50 million in three years. Investors can smell bullshit. Start small. Even though your big goal could be to run an organization with fifty divisions and a thousand employees, first prove you can perform miracles with a small, focused team or by yourself.

Avoid sucking-up and trying too hard to be friends with the investor. At the end of the day, this is business and you should keep it professional. Also, check your attitude at the door and have a slice of humble pie. You are basically begging these people for money. It's very rare that you're going to be lauded for "telling it like it is" to an investor who is likely older and wiser than you. Try listening an equal or greater amount of time than you speak. Stand up for yourself when appropriate, but don't get sassy. Display confidence, not arrogance. Be passionate and pepper in a personal anecdote here and there if it helps illustrate your capabilities.

Last but not least, learn something about the investor. Who are the people you are meeting, what have they done, who have they invested in before? Knowledge is power and you never know what nugget of information will win you the investment deal of a lifetime.

EXERCISE: Write your pitch to an investor. Then, practice on a friend.

EXERCISE: Identify five potential investors through your friends and family, extended network, or by asking other business people.

FUNDING METHOD #9:

TAKE ON A LOAN

A loan is borrowed money from the bank, paid back with interest by a deadline. The average small business loan is about $150,000, according to whitehouse.gov. Loans are often used for starting brick-and-mortar businesses, like a restaurant, a hair salon, or a grocery store. When you sign a loan agreement, you are signing a legal contract that can give the bank authority to seize your property or other collateral, if you fail to repay. Collateral is sometimes called a "personal guarantee." Don't be confused by the politically correct legalese—you are still giving the bank the right to seize your car, your house, or personal property. Before you apply for a loan, ask yourself:

- Is there any other way you can raise or earn this money?
- Can you reduce the size of the loan request? How?
- Are you completely sure that you will be able to pay the loan back? How will you do this?
- Are you willing to pay the interest rate (possibly between 7 and 8 percent)? How will you do this?
- Are you willing to be in debt until you repay the loan?
- Are you willing to face the repercussions if you fail to pay back the loan? What's your worst-case scenario plan?

How to Get a Loan

Before you seek a loan, talk to people who have taken and successfully repaid their loans. Ask for their input on your situation. Talk to financial professionals (someone other than your preferred lending institution) for their advice.

Loans require a stellar credit history so pay credit, auto, home, insurance, and other bills on time. Institutions assume you will handle business finances the same as personal finances. As you build up your credit score, work on a detailed business plan.

Once you're ready to seek a loan, go to a bank where you already have an account, a mortgage, or another loan. Having history with an institution will increase their trust because they have access to your financial records. Arrange a meeting with a loan officer at your bank, and be sure to ask if you qualify for a low-interest loan. There may be low-interest loans available to businesses that are minority-owned, women-owned, veteran-owned, GLBTQ-owned, or persons-with-disabilities-owned. At the loan meeting, be prepared for the following questions:

- Why do you need a loan?
- What specific purchases do you need to make? From who?
- What are your other sources of funding or debts?
- Who is the management team?

If you are granted a loan, be extremely wary about offering collateral. You never know what life might throw at you. Even the best laid business plans can go awry due to personal injuries, tragedy, or surprises.

FUNDRAISING METHOD #10:
TO CHARGE IT OR NOT TO CHARGE IT?

The short answer: no. Credit cards are a very risky way to fund a dream. Use a credit card only if you are financially stable and trying to build up a credit score. Make sure whatever purchases you make on the card can be paid off in full at the end of the month.

Credit cards promote a dangerous attitude of "spend now, find a way to pay later," and have high-interest rates. The longer purchases linger, unpaid on your credit card bill, the more interest they rack up. Paying the minimum on your balance for an extended period of time can lead to paying double the original purchase price. Credit cards can also come with other hidden costs like an annual fee, a flat yearly charge, a membership fee, or a finance charge, all in addition to interest you have to pay. Don't drown your dreams in debt. Build your dream on a more stable foundation than a plastic credit card.

WHAT ABOUT MY SAVINGS?

You should also exercise caution when using your savings to fund a dream. This is common sense, but it must be said: never invest all of your savings into a dream. If you do want to use some savings, make sure you have a sizeable chunk of change left over in your bank account. Most experts recommend having at least six month's worth of living expenses saved up at all times. Never spend more than you're willing to lose. The money you invest has no guarantee of return.

SUMMARY POINTS:

- A day job is the most secure, stable, and consistent way to raise funds for your dream and cover living expenses. Hold on to your day job while you work on your dream.

- You can work a weird, wacky, one-time gig to bring in some quick and easy cash for your dream. Or, seek out a more stable option like babysitting, bartending, or doing seasonal work.

- Use fundraising events, raffles, and auctions to get donors together and encourage giving.

- Crowdsourcing websites give you an online platform to raise money for your dream. Be ready to spend a lot of time soliciting donations from your extended network.

- Sponsorships and in-kind donations can partially fund your dream, in return for advertising a brand.

- If more education is needed, apply for scholarships or fellowships.

- Pick up the grant-writing books we recommended to write a winning proposal.

- Contests are a great way to organize your ideas, generate publicity, and compete for cash.

- Investors want to see *your* investment. Show them you are committed and passionate to win their support.

- If you're building a brick-and-mortar business you can consider a loan. Just be cautious about offering collateral.

- Avoid funding your dream with a credit card.

- Never dump your life's savings into a dream. Be smart, don't risk too much, and always have backup funds.

CHAPTER 9:
FIGHTING AGAINST YOURSELF

You have to stay motivated.

"When you look for things in life like love, meaning, motivation, it implies they are sitting behind a tree or under a rock. The most successful people in life recognize that in life they create their own love, they manufacture their own meaning, they generate their own motivation."

—Neil deGrasse Tyson

The beginning of a project is usually exhilarating. There are a million tasks to complete, new skills to learn, people to talk to, and lots of big ideas to flesh out. Then, motivation begins to wane during the transition from grand scheme to daily details. Your progress on your homerun idea for a website screeches to a halt as you spend days debugging HTML code. You get bogged down in revisions of your novel's threadbare plot and never want to look at it again. You begin to dread the challenges of the day. Responding to e-mails and filling out more paperwork makes you want to scream. Going back for revisions for the fifth time induces tears. You've got weeks of long nights ahead of you, with no respite in sight. This is a critical time in a dreamer's journey. It's sink or swim. Either push through to the end or lose motivation and give up. What will your story be?

Did you have a good idea for an invention that you designed but never finished? Or, did you bring your product to market and launch a thriving business? Did your wood carving collect dust, half finished in your studio? Or, did you show it at a gallery and sell to a collector? Did you leave a grant proposal to mold in your desk drawer? Or, did you submit it and win state funding for your after-school program?

Let's look at ways to stay motivated and cross the bridge from halfway to completion by:

1. Creating Your Own Gold Stars
2. Eliminating Habitual Procrastination
3. Expanding Your Support Network
4. Recharging to Avoid Burnout
5. Realizing the Grass is Not Greener
5. Overcoming Perfectionist Tendencies

CREATING YOUR OWN GOLD STARS

We are a culture obsessed with quick and visible results and rewards. We have recipes for thirty-minute meals, twelve-week crash diet plans, and five-minute ab workouts to get you ripped, fast. In this quick-fix, result-oriented cultural climate, it can be discouraging to work on your dream for months with nothing to show for it. You're broke, no one knows what you're doing, and you have yet to make an impact. It can be hard to keep pushing on without any reward.

If you feel your motivation dwindling, focus on the intangible rewards, skills, or experiences you have gained. Maybe you improved editing skills, learned how to write a business plan, pitched your idea to a potential investor, changed your work habits, wrote fifty pages, spoke in front of ten people, or completed a class. It's important to celebrate what you've gained. Throw yourself a party, make an award, or post a list of accomplishments above your workspace. Sounds corny, but it works. We are visual creatures and we all need a gold star every now and then.

You can also bribe yourself into work with rewards. Here are eight potential prizes you can treat yourself with:

Daily reward: If I write 2,000 words today, I can treat myself to frozen yogurt.

Weekly reward: If I meet all of my goals this week, I can go to the movies on Sunday.

Completion reward: I'll get a massage once I finish my rough draft.

Delayed satisfaction: Once I finish this task, I can watch TV for a half hour.

Upgrade reward: If I complete all the action items on my list, I'll get a bouquet of flowers for my desk, a reusable mug for the local coffee shop where I do work, or a new set of pens.

Consistency reward: If I work six days this week, I can go to the beach all day Sunday.

Social reward: To make work more fun today, a friend and I will meet at a coffee shop to knock out our to-do lists together.

EXERCISE: List five rewards that would motivate you to do work.

EXERCISE: Make a list of skills you've gained or experiences you're proud of so far. Post this list above your workspace.

EXERCISE: Make your own award. Today, print out a certificate or create an award that celebrates your first prototype, draft, or a skill you improved. For example, Most Improved in Video Editing, Underdog Award for Getting Funded, or Most Likely to Succeed. Post this where you work.

ELIMINATING HABITUAL PROCRASTINATION

Dreams have long-term rewards. The problem is many of us are short-term pleasure junkies. We blow off work for what is easy, fun, and instantly obtainable. Watching television, playing a video game, or eating provides an immediate rush of endorphins that work does not. However, as you waste more time, the initial pleasure buzz wears off. The anxiety builds as you think about the tasks you are avoiding. Soon, the feelings of guilt start to creep in. Some chronic procrastinators will desperately try to get their initial pleasure rush back: "I'll feel better after one more round of Angry Birds! Or, one more rerun of *The Office!*" Eventually, you shut off the TV and limp back to your work, tail between your legs. Where has the time gone?

How to Cure Common Forms of Procrastination

Type of Procrastination	Cure
Internet browsing: online shopping, the blogosphere, and social media.	Use Internet-blocking software to curb your time online. Try out the following programs: FB Limiter, Leechblock, Anti-Social, StayFocusd, or JDarkRoom
The Google Disease: You can't remember a minor detail (an actor's name, piece of trivia, the author of an article you read, population statistics for Los Angeles), and you have to look it up *right now* or it will bug you until you know.	Jot the idea down. Come back to it later, once work is complete, if it's actually important.
Distracting environment: Easy access to TV, the fridge, or your cell phone makes it impossible to stay focused.	Get out of the house, hunker down in the library, unplug or hide electronics.
Socialite Syndrome: You were supposed to go home and tinker with the sound levels on your demo, but then a coworker invites you out for office happy hour. Socializing seems more fun than sound editing, so you go. By the time you get home, you're too tired to do anything but crash into bed.	Use socializing as a reward. For example, "If I go home right away and do work, I can meet my friend for a late dinner." If you want to socialize at night, you must wake up early to get work done.
Substance abuse: One more beer before I start writing. (Hemingway did it!) I need to get high before I play music. (Hendrix did it!) One more bump and I'll hit the trading floor. (Gordon Gekko did it!)	Don't buy into the myth that you need drugs or alcohol to alter your mind and work on your dream. Hemingway killed himself, Hendrix OD'd, and Gekko got sent to the slammer. If you find yourself using alcohol or other substances to escape reality or put off tasks, seek professional help.

Productive Procrastination

Some of us are productive procrastinators. We tell ourselves we will work on our dream once we: walk the dog, do the dishes, fold the laundry, clean the bathroom, sort the mail, pay the bills, run to the grocery store, stop at the post office, pick up a new bottle of shampoo, or spend two hours crafting a fancy dinner.

We enjoy this kind of procrastination because it's relatively guilt free. After all, you feel accomplished when you spend a whole day checking items off a to-do list. Don't be fooled by productive procrastination. You might have the cleanest house in the world, but what's it worth if your dream is covered in dust and cobwebs?

Chores are important and necessary, but working on your dream is urgent. Treat it as such and give your dreams priority above mundane household tasks. Wait until your chores need to be addressed: don't do laundry until the hamper's full, wait until the carpet looks dirty to whip out the vacuum, and combine errands to avoid multiple trips. Your time is the most important resource you have. Spend it on your dream, not scrubbing the floor.

EXERCISE: Answer the following: What are your three go-to forms of procrastination? Why do you engage in these particular activities? How do you feel as you do them? How do you feel after you do them?

EXERCISE: Lights out! Shut down all electronics for a self-prescribed amount of time. How does your productivity increase without checking websites, your cell phone buzzing, or the TV blaring in the background?

EXPANDING YOUR SUPPORT NETWORK

Isolation can kill motivation. We all need cheerleaders and sympathizers. Now is the time to expand your Circle of Trust to include other people chasing their dreams. Surround yourself with other passionate individuals to spark new ideas, reaffirm your love for a project, or ignite a healthy competitive streak. Are any of your friends pursuing their dream or hatching plans? Will they lend you their ears for a venting session every now and then? Getting a passion project off the ground can be exhausting and sometimes you just need to complain. Enlist a buddy who will understand your struggles and frustrations. Or, try searching online for support forums, Facebook groups, or e-mail listservs.

RECHARGING TO AVOID BURNOUT

Dreams require mining the depths of your mental, emotional, and physical energy. As you pour more into your work, make it a point to relax and recharge. Healthy sleeping habits, a balanced diet, and exercise are critical to staying sane, happy, and energized. Work becomes a lot more difficult when you're running on three hours of sleep, surviving on Top Ramen dinners, and shunning sunlight. You're not superhuman. You will accomplish more when fully rested and not crazed on caffeine and lack of sleep. Overstimulation and over-scheduling is a recipe for burnout. Here are some healthy and low-cost ways to relax, recharge, and rejuvenate:

Take a walk alone

Write in a journal

Go to the library and read a book for an hour

Go for a run or hike

Take a nap

Take a blanket to a park and lay out in the sunshine

Write a letter to a friend

Try to meditate

Volunteer—focusing on others can put your life into perspective

Take a hot bath

Put on some music and dance

Draw, paint, or use Play-Doh to make mini-sculptures

Visit a museum or exhibit

Listen to a favorite song

Drive to a store, church, school, or park you've always wanted to visit and check out the space

Take yourself on a date—get lunch, coffee, or a snack alone

Take a yoga class

Play an instrument

See a lecture or speaker

Sit in a crowded area with a notebook and take notes on the people and scenery

Go see a live musical performance or theater piece

Read the newspaper every day for a week

Make a collage out of old photographs and magazines

Cook or bake

Paint a piece of furniture

Complete a puzzle, Sudoku, or crossword

Fix or mend something—using the mechanical side of your brain can get the gears clicking

Laugh—watch a funny movie or show, read a funny book, blog or article, or, spend time with a friend who makes you crack up

Play a board game—strategizing and competing will get the blood flowing to a stale mind

Play an outdoor game—tennis, soccer, basketball

Go for a walk or run in a new-to-you neighborhood or trail

Garden or plant something

Keep an inspiration folder on your computer, filled with bookmarks of photos, articles or websites you like. You can also make a physical inspiration folder with magazine or newspaper clippings, old photos, ticket stubs, and drawings. When you're feeling burned out, flip through the file for instant inspiration.

REALIZING THE GRASS IS NOT GREENER

A loss of motivation might make you yearn for the old days when you weren't working on a challenging project, double checking your budget, or juggling dream work with family duties and a day job. Remember when you only had to worry about punching the clock and collecting a paycheck every two weeks?

Looking at the past through rose-colored glasses is a coping mechanism to deal with difficulty. In truth, hindsight and nostalgia distort memories, cover up ugly details, and make things seem better than they really were. You chose to chase your dream for a reason: something was missing and you wanted more. Don't delude yourself into thinking life used to be perfect. Embrace the present. Struggle builds character and sweetens victory.

EXERCISE: Make a vision board. Create a collage of pictures and words that represent all the things you want. Post your vision board in a place you see every day to remind you why you are working so hard.

OVERCOMING PERFECTIONIST TENDENCIES

Endless editing, reworking, tweaking, redesigning—it all can bring your progress to a standstill and kill your motivation. Perfectionism is the voice that whispers in our ear "if you just go back one more time, then it will be perfect." Do you have any of the following perfectionist tendencies?

- You have trouble overlooking minor imperfections in your work.
- You have to get it right the first time, every time.
- You keep raising the bar, holding yourself to higher and higher standards.

- You worry that if you do succeed you won't be able to maintain your success.
- You believe that when you fail, it's time to quit. You failed for a reason, and the reason is you're not good enough.
- You constantly think about past mistakes—it's hard to let them go.
- You embrace all-or-nothing thinking. You won or lost. You are the best or the worst. You are hard working or lazy. You are brilliant or stupid.
- You set unrealistic deadlines or take on way too many responsibilities.

Imperfection, Guaranteed

Perfection is impossible. Again, you're not superhuman. To overcome perfectionism you must start by accepting yourself as a less-than-perfect being. This means setting realistic expectations for both the quality and quantity of the work you do. Allow your work to be good, not great. Give yourself an extra week for a big project. Don't bite off more than you can chew.

There is a difference between perfection and high quality. People who do high-quality work are comfortable making mistakes and view them as part of the learning process. They are able to let go of their work, make it public, and open themselves up to praise and disapproval. People who do high-quality work enjoy the fruits of their labor and let negative reviews roll off their shoulders. Perfectionists, on the other hand, struggle to enjoy the results of their work and crumble at the first hint of criticism. If you want to accomplish anything in life, strive to be the person who does high-quality work, not perfect work.

When to Let Go of Your Work

At some point, it will be time to send your work off into the world. Your manuscript will be ready for review, your album will be mixed and mastered, or you will be ready to share your invention with manufacturers. Here are some general guidelines to help you decide when to let go of your work:

- Have you had multiple friends and colleagues review your work and provide advice for improvement?
- Have you had at least one mentor or professional look at your work?
- Have you revised your work multiple times based on the feedback you received?
- Have you revised your work multiple times, specifically looking for and fixing technical details—proofreading, spelling, grammar, glitches, skips, defects, bugs, or flaws?
- Have you done a test run of your product or service with potential customers? Try to do a small trial before a big launch.
- Do you feel like you've given your best effort to this project and improved it as much as you can?

If you really feel like you've done your absolute best, there is no need to hold on to your project any longer. Every day you wait is just one more delay on the road to success.

SUMMARY POINTS

- Create visual reminders of your progress to increase motivation. Create a running list of achievements and treat yourself with some rewards.

- Don't trick yourself into thinking productive procrastination, chores, or busy work is getting you any closer to your dreams.

- Surround yourself with fellow dream chasers to provide advice, spark ideas, and ignite a competitive fire in you. Best of all, you can complain to them!

- Avoid burnout, stick to healthy habits, and devote at least one hour per week to creative replenishment or relaxing.

- The grass is not always greener. Stop pining for the past and focus on the benefits of the present.

- Do high-quality, not "perfect" work. Learn to let go.

CHAPTER 10:

PREPARE FOR TAKEOFF

"Whatever we possess becomes of
double value when we have the
opportunity of sharing it with others."

—Jean-Nicolas Bouilly

You've tightened the screws, polished your prose, and triple-checked your work with microscopic intensity. It's time for takeoff. This could mean launching your business or nonprofit, sending out a demo or portfolio, going to an interview at your dream company, or submitting your work to a conference, festival, gallery, or publisher. Let's prepare to share by:

1. Finding Your Inner Salesperson
2. Finding Your Ideal Customer
3. Defining Your Brand
3. Creating and Customizing a Sales Pitch
4. Spreading the Word

FINDING YOUR INNER SALESPERSON

Hey, artists, don't skip this chapter! Selling is the final step of the creative process. Just like a businessperson, you need to find your ideal customer, present your pitch, and be fairly compensated. Many artists struggle with salesmanship because it seems disingenuous and difficult. But if you want to earn a living as an artist, you have to sell your art. Otherwise, it's just a hobby. If you want to book concerts, performances, or film screenings, you need to identify venues that will pay you to play. If you want to sell a script or story, you must identify agents, producers, and publishers. If you want a buyer for your latest painting, contact galleries, fairs, stores, or private collectors. In this chapter, we'll give you the tools you need to unleash your inner salesperson and earn profit from your work.

FINDING YOUR IDEAL CUSTOMER

Define your ideal customer by answering the following:

- What type of person would hire you or purchase from you?
- What do they look like?
- How old are they?
- Where do they live?
- What do they do for a living?
- What do they like about their job? Dislike?
- What do they do for fun?
- What are their goals?
- What are their problems?
- What do they value?
- What do they spend disposable income on?
- Where do they hang out (at a gym, on Twitter, or independently owned stores)?
- What lifestyle trends are they interested in?
- What types of media, publicity, or advertising do they respond to?
- Why would your customer want your product or service?
- Where would your ideal customer be likely to purchase your product or service?
- Why would a customer buy your product over a competitor's?

DEFINING YOUR BRAND

Once you hone in on a target customer, you need to craft a brand that appeals to them. Sugar Taylor is the Creative Director of DIYva Designs, an event-planning company. She shared the following advice about branding: "You have to look at every decision you make as a representation of your brand. Every detail counts—website design, the words you choose, little things like stationery, the way you market, and especially the people on your team. People are the most

166 I BUILD YOUR DREAMS

important part of your brand. Branding is about being authentic and then projecting that authentic image to the world."

Brands exist in the mind. Your brand is the ideas, images, and emotions people associate with your work. Your brand consists of—logo, your name, color choices, website design, social media, messaging, the way you advertise, your price, the design and packaging of your product, clothing choices and personal appearance (if you're in the public eye), business card design, the materials you use to make your products, your ethics and sustainability practices, your mission statement, and the people you partner with, employ, and do business with. All of these pieces form a cohesive picture that tells the customer who you are, what you do, and what you stand for.

What Makes Your Brand Special?

As marketing expert Laura Ries said, "Brands that try to appeal to everyone end up appealing to no one." Successful brands get their start by appealing to a small, target audience. They become a specialist, an expert in one category. Under Armour shirts were targeted to athletes. Apple products were for design-geeks and tech-nerds. Clif Bars were for outdoor adventurers.

People respond to companies that were created especially for them. What are you a specialist in? Craft your image accordingly. Under Armour ads show serious athletes dripping sweat, Apple's marketing is simple and sleek, and Clif Bars have mountain climbers on their wrappers.

Creative types cultivate a brand image as well. Stephen King has creepy artwork on his book covers and wrought-iron gargoyles and spiderwebs on the gate to his house. Lady Gaga calls her fans "little monsters" and dresses like one herself. Jimmy Buffet, with his unbuttoned Hawaiian shirt and margarita in hand, has the market cornered on the beach bum lifestyle. As an artist or businessperson, your brand should be a natural extension of yourself.

EXERCISE: Build your brand. What's your niche? How can you appeal to this niche with your branding? Describe how your brand will be reflected through each of the following:

- Name of brand
- Logo
- Color choices
- Website design
- Social media
- Messaging
- Advertising

- Design and packaging of product
- Personal appearance (if you're in the public eye)
- Business card design
- Materials used to make your products
- Ethics and sustainability practices
- Mission statement
- People you partner with, employ, and do business with

What's Your Price?

The cost of your product or service is also a part of your brand, so set an appealing price that resonates with your target audience. Is your brand a great deal? Is your brand honest, handcrafted, and high quality? Numbers have a psychological effect. Odd numbers, like $9.99, imply a bargain. Even numbers generally convey quality and sophistication. To determine your price, talk to real people who fit your vision of an ideal customer, do a poll, ask your social network, or set up a survey. Ask people:

- How much have they paid for similar products or services?
- If they were you, how much would they charge?
- Are they looking for a great deal or are they willing to pay a little bit more for higher quality and better service? Or are they somewhere in the middle?

You can also use the Rule of Three to get an idea of what price range you fall into. Look at three similar products or services to determine the average price. Start small. Don't compare your price to industry veterans who have earned the right to charge more or who can undercut competition with their huge volume of sales.

EXERCISE: What's your price? Research your ideal customer to see how much they will pay, use the Rule of Three, and be sure to account for the psychological effects of numbers. Pick a price that will be profitable.

CREATING AND CUSTOMIZING A SALES PITCH

What words will move money from your customer's pocket to your own? You need a pitch. Your pitch should simply answer the following questions: What are you selling, what type of person do you appeal to, and why should someone buy your product or service? "We sell gluten-free trail mix for active people on-the-go. . . . We offer one-day guided tours of the Finger Lakes to visit craft wineries, family-owned restaurants, and mom-and-pop dairy farms. . . . Our zine publishes high-quality photographs and poems by the LGBTQ community."

If you're e-mailing your pitch to a potential customer or employer, include the following elements:

Introduction: What's your name and organization?

Logline: Describe your organization, product, or service in a sentence. (Make it specific—remember people love specialists, not generalists. What is unique?)

Do Your Homework, Customization Counts! Make the recipient feel special. Avoid mass e-mails addressed "Dear Sir or Madam." It's just lazy. With the Internet, there is no excuse for not adding a personal touch: "Hi Steve, I came across your name in connection with _____ and I thought you might see similar potential in my work. . . . Hi Michele, I really admired the work you did on _____ and would love for you to take a look at my project. . . . Hi Mel, I really enjoyed your article in _____ and wanted to connect with you about _____."

Benefits of your product or service: Why would someone want this? What problems are you solving or improving?

Appeal to the heart or head: Why do you believe in your mission?

Qualifications and testimony: This is where you can name-drop, list any endorsements, positive reviews, or qualifications. "I've been studying this for five years. . . . I've worked with six other businesses in town. . . . You can check out the article about me in the *Sunday Times*."

Where can someone purchase or learn more? End your pitch with a call to action or provide an outlet for further conversation. Sign off with your contact information, promote your website, toss in your Twitter handle, plug the store or event you'll be seen at next week, or give them a coupon for their next visit.

Ring, Ring

You can also pitch over the phone. Since e-mail is *de rigueur*, a phone call seems urgent and important in comparison. It's a lot harder to ignore a ringing phone than it is to send an e-mail to the trash bin. Phone calls have a personal touch and allow you to control the tone, unlike an e-mail where your words can be misconstrued. After someone's heard your voice and chatted for a few minutes, they feel like they know the person behind the website, e-mail, or business card.

Make sure to call during the right time of day. Don't make pitches early in the morning, lunch (11:30–2 p.m.), or after 4 p.m. Ditto for Mondays. No one likes to deal with anything, let alone a sales pitch, on a Monday. Friday afternoons and the days before and after holidays are trouble, too.

Before calling, rehearse answers to common questions. Do a few test runs with a friend to nail your performance. Remember the mantra: fake it till you make it. If you sound confident, people will believe in what you say. If you have a tendency to ramble, practice pitching in under two minutes. Convey the essential details, cut the fluff. If your pitch could be enhanced with a presentation, set up a meeting. Or, if it seems appropriate, drop by when they're not too busy.

SPREADING THE WORD

Brands are born through publicity. For start-ups and newcomers, publicity is a free and effective way to create a buzz and ramps up sales. Publicity is media attention: an article about an author's new bestselling book, a guest appearance on a podcast, or a blog post about someone starting their own television show. The media is constantly looking for news, entertainment, and useful information. Want publicity? Give them something to write about.

- Are you offering a product or service that has never been seen before?
- Could the media outlet be the first to review your product, service, or performance?
- Are you part of a trend?
- Are you addressing an overlooked problem?
- Are you reaching an untapped or underserved market?
- Are you doing something unique, compared to your competitors?
- Are you running a special, promotion, or contest?
- Could your story inspire others? Is there a human-interest angle?
- Have you been featured in other media outlets? (Publicity begets more publicity.)
- Can you stage a publicity stunt? You can do something wild or noteworthy like the entrepreneur who flew around the world in a red hot air balloon to announce his latest tourism venture. . . . The animal rights activist group that ambushes fur-wearing starlets on the red carpet with paint and tofu pies to the face. . . . Or, the New Orleanian nonprofit founder we met who painted himself gold, dressed up like the Saints quarterback, and posed for pictures in the French Quarter to raise money.

EXERCISE: Why would a media outlet want to share your story? Come up with three story angles.

EXERCISE: Identify potential publicity outlets. Answer the following:

What are three local newspapers you can contact?
What are seven blogs you can contact?
What are three magazines you can contact?
Who are three tastemakers (influential and popular people) in your industry?
What are six radio shows or podcasts you can try to go on?
What are three events that would be great to be seen at this year?

EXERCISE: Write a press release that you can send to publicity outlets. Once complete, send out your press release to the media outlets you just listed. Customization counts. **Note:** You might not need to send a formal press release to a blog or podcast.

Press Release Example

For Immediate Release   Contact: Alexis Irvin, 555-555-5555
E-mail: TheDreamShareProject@gmail.com
Website: www.thedreamshareproject.com

Howard County Residents Create Documentary Film

LAUREL, MD., (May 25, 2011) *The Dream Share Project* is a feature length documentary film about learning what it means to chase a dream, currently in post-production by local Howard County residents Chip Hiden and Alexis Irvin.

Hiden and Irvin took off on a three-month coast-to-coast road trip in September 2010 with a plan to interview successful people who were chasing their dreams. Armed with Flip cameras, the duo documented their travel adventures and over thirty inspirational interviews, having had no previous filmmaking experience.

The film follows the recent college graduates as they learn about discovering one's passion, committing to a dream, dealing with setbacks, and redefining success for the Millennial generation.

Interviews included an Olympic skier, an original Latin Kings of Comedy comedian, a renowned slam poet, a *Project Runway* contestant, the producer of the PBS show *Austin City Limits*, the founder of the South by Southwest Festival, and the CEO and founder of Feelgoodz Flip Flops. Interview clips can be found on thedreamshareproject.com.

The goal of *The Dream Share Project* film is to inspire and incite young people to take action and follow their dreams.

Returning home at the end of November 2010, Hiden and Irvin immediately launched into editing their footage into a film.

The Dream Share Project was selected to join the Creative Activist Program, run by the Creative Visions Foundation. The Creative Visions Foundation supports activists who use media and the arts to create positive change in the world.

Call Don Draper

Advertising can be expensive, especially for beginners who are still recouping high startup costs or struggling to turn a profit. Before you think about paying for advertising, make sure you've exhausted all options for publicity. Advertising is usually helpful for businesses once they have rode out their publicity wave. Or, they need to maintain their status as a major brand and differentiate from a competitor, like the "I'm a PC, not a Mac" ad campaign.

Advertising can be used to announce grand openings, product launches, new locations, discounts, coupons, specials, and sales. Keep in mind that the medium you choose to advertise with will reflect your brand's image—a cheap-looking flyer or TV spot can do more harm than good. Have a few friends or customers give you an honest opinion of your ad before launching a campaign. Great advertisements appeal to the ideal customer with the perfect blend of art and persuasion. As Howard Gossage, advertising guru and real life Mad Man, said: "The real fact of the matter is that nobody reads ads. People read what interests them, and sometimes it's an ad."

The New Face of Advertising

Services like Groupon, Google ads, Facebook ads, and Search Engine Optimization are revamping the way we advertise. If you have a website or a product you want to sell online, you need to become familiar with these services.

Daily-deal services like Groupon and Living Social deliver e-mail coupons for local businesses. These sites let you target lots of potential customers in a specific region or city. Daily-deal services require you to offer a severe discount on a product or service, sometimes as much as 50 percent. You can expect a rush of business, but make sure your staffing and inventory can handle it. If you sell too much, too cheaply, you might end up with empty shelves, empty coffers, and an overwhelmed staff. If you want to use a daily-deal site, discount an item that has a high profit margin so you don't lose your shirt on every sale. Or, look at your discounted item as a loss-leader and push another full-priced product to make up the difference. Just know that daily-deal campaigns tend to attract clientele prone to bargain-hunting. Most are just looking for a cheap, one-time experience.

Pay-Per-Click (PPC) services like Google Adsense allow you to write ads that show up in online searches based on the keywords you choose. As a result, your ad reaches people as they are actively searching for products or services like yours. For example, someone searches for a lawyer and your firm's ad shows up. To get started, write your ad, choose the search terms that describe your product or service, and then set a daily or monthly budget. You pay the PPC service a small fee each time someone clicks your ad. Monitor how many sales your PPC campaign generates and adjust your advertising budget accordingly. Be warned, there are some problems with PPC: MediaMind, an Internet advertising research firm, estimates the click rate of Internet ads is only 0.09%. Also, people might be able to find your website without a PPC ad. Do you really need to pay a dollar per click?

One way to ensure that people can find your website without PPC is Search Engine Optimization (SEO). SEO helps increase your website's ranking in search engine results by adding metadata and hidden keywords to your website. Many advertising firms and web designers offer SEO services for a price, but you can probably figure it out yourself if you're tech-savvy. Make sure your keywords match your services and don't try to steal traffic with misleading words and phrases. Your visitors won't appreciate being deceived and some search engines penalize shady SEO practices.

Success in 140 Characters or Less

Social media lets you connect and interact with customers, offer entertainment or information, and promote products, sales, and discounts. If your website or social media offers fresh, relevant, or fun content, customers will come back for more. People want consistency, so make it a point to update your social media platforms regularly: a tweet every day around lunch, a blog post every Monday morning, or a new YouTube video every month. Content is king.

Social media shouldn't be used solely as a vehicle for sales, profit, and shameless self-promotion. Instead, use social media to make authentic connections with potential customers, make friends with others in your industry, and increase visibility. One of our friends, @IamChrisTodd, is an aspiring comedy writer and a Twitter-addict. He connected with @IFCtv and was offered the chance to live-tweet his comic musings on the TV show *Portlandia*. Social media let him get his foot in the door of the comedic world.

To be effective, become a part of the online community surrounding your product or service. Comment and interact on other blogs, websites, and social media sites. Join the conversation. Don't let a vocal commenter, poster, or tweeter go unnoticed or unappreciated. Give props to other people's work. They might just do the same for you.

EXERCISE:

List five ways you will use Facebook to promote your brand.

List five ways you will use Twitter to promote your brand.

List five ways you will use other services to promote your brand (Pinterest, LinkedIn, Instagram, Reddit, Tumblr).

List five video ideas for YouTube or Vimeo.

List five blog topics you could write about.

SUMMARY POINTS

• Be a specialist.

• Customize your brand, pitch, and publicity to appeal to your niche.

• Set a competitive and profitable price using the Rule of Three. What does your price say about your brand?

• Pick up the phone, pull off a publicity stunt, or chirp in the Twittersphere to create a buzz and put your name on the map.

CHAPTER 11:
HIT, STAY, FOLD

Strategize to deal with failure,
criticism, and rejection.

"I haven't failed, I've found 10,000
ways that don't work."

—Thomas Edison

Rejection is par-for-the-course when you're pursuing what you love. Twelve publishers rejected J. K. Rowling's *Harry Potter* manuscript. A record label famously told The Beatles: "Guitar groups are on the way out," and "The Beatles have no future in show business." Henry Ford had five failed businesses before he started the Ford Motor Company. Lucille Ball was sent home from acting school because her teachers told her she was too shy. Steve Jobs was fired from Apple in 1985. Michael Jordan was cut from his high school basketball team. Albert Einstein was expelled from elementary school and rejected from Zurich Polytechnic School. Abraham Lincoln lost multiple elections before becoming president. Oprah Winfrey was fired from her job as a television news reporter after being told she was "unfit for TV."

Titans of industry, stars of the stage, great-thinkers, and world-changers—they've all been rejected and made to look like fools. They kept moving. Let's discuss how you can do the same. We will explore:

1. What Criticism Looks Like
2. What Rejection Looks Like
3. The Five Stages of Rejection and Criticism
4. Avoiding a Shame Spiral
5. Strategies for Dealing with Rejection: Stay, Hit, or Fold
6. Creating Your Own Luck

WHAT CRITICISM LOOKS LIKE

Sharing your work invites opinions. Criticism can be good, bad, and ugly. Good criticism might sting, but after the initial pain subsides, it clears the way for improvements. Nasty criticism is self-serving, unnecessarily harsh, or just plain unfair. Watch out for these types of criticism:

Sneaky, Snarky: A critique veiled as a question or a commentary. "Can you explain the choice you made to use low-quality photos and sound?"

Holier than Thou: A critique that unfairly reduces the importance of your work. "It's great that your nonprofit works with homeless people, but shouldn't you focus on something more important like AIDS, cancer, or the environment?"

The Deconstructionist: A critique that devolves into philosophical ramblings. "I understand that your work is supposed to help people, but the question is, how does this *really* help people? How do any of us really help anyone? Is it with words? Deeds? Books? Community initiatives?"

Wet Blanket Statements: A critique that over-generalizes. "This is the worst idea I have ever heard."

Jealous Jibe: "Your book proposal is alright, but why should you write a book? You just run a blog, I could do that!"

The High and Mighty: "As someone with a very refined sense of taste, I can tell you this is low class."

Learn to differentiate between constructive and nasty criticism. Take what's helpful from a critique and toss aside the blanket statements, jealous jibes, and philosophical rants. Remember, criticism is subjective. Most of the time, a critique is simply the result of a difference of opinion or personal taste. You can't please everybody.

Also, keep in mind that people tend to offer criticism much more than they offer praise. The White House Office of Consumer Affairs found that, on average, a dissatisfied customer will tell 9–15 people about their negative experience. A happy and satisfied customer will only tell 4–6 people about their positive experience. Everyone is a critic. You are a creator.

EXERCISE: After being criticized, answer the following:
- Analyze the comments you got. Were they constructive, nasty, or a mixture?
- What was helpful in the critique?
- What was just hurtful?
- What changes do you want to make based on the criticism?

WHAT REJECTION LOOKS LIKE

In addition to being critiqued, you may just get flat out rejected. Rejection wears many masks, each with their own particularly ugly features:

The Shut Out: You never get a response to your pitch, demo, or query—even after multiple follow-up calls.

The Hard No: A curt rejection with no explanation. "No thank you, please do not contact us again."

The Polite Decline: A rejection with a reason. "This is great but it doesn't fit our company vision. . . . We love it, but we don't have the money for a project like this right now."

The Nasty No: A rejection with a reason that hurts your feelings. "This sounds too risky, I don't think you have the talent to pull it off."

Laser Accuracy: A deep-cutting rejection based on a weakness you were acutely aware of. For example, you suspected the characters in your screenplay were underdeveloped, and your script was rejected for that very reason.

THE FIVE STAGES OF REJECTION AND CRITICISM

Coping with the emotional fallout of a rejection or harsh critique is similar to the five stages of grief and loss.

First, you deny. "I can't believe Lynn told me to do a second draft, I thought she was going to love this. . . . I can't believe I didn't get promoted, I was the best candidate. . . . I can't believe that the investor hasn't gotten back to me, they must have missed my e-mail."

Next, you get angry. You imagine calling Lynn to yell at her. You type out an angry e-mail, bashing your employer. You contemplate writing something rude online about your potential investor.

Now, you try to bargain. If I can just explain my idea again to Lynn, maybe she'll understand it better. If I could only talk to my employer one more time, I could show them how I'm the ideal candidate for the promotion. If I send my pitch again and just ask for less money, maybe the investor will consider me.

Then, depression might follow. What's the point of even trying to re-do this? Why do I even go to work anymore if I have no hope of moving up? Why should I even start a business if I can't get one person to invest in my idea?

Finally, acceptance. I can look at Lynn's suggestions again, make changes based on the ones I agree with, and do a second draft. I'll work harder than ever and try again for the promotion or search for an employer who will better appreciate my skills. I can revise my business plan and reach out to new investors. Meanwhile, I'll explore creative ways to raise funds.

Don't be reactionary when you've been rejected or criticized. Give yourself a day or two to feel hurt and go through the stages of rejection. Once the pain has settled, you can move onto the acceptance stage and look at your options with clear eyes and a level head.

EXERCISE: Write an essay responding to a recent rejection or criticism that really upset you. Write down all of your negative thoughts. When you're done, destroy the essay, along with your bad mood.

EXERCISE: Make rejection your ally, not your enemy. Rejection or criticism can be a teacher. What are three things you can learn from a recent rejection or criticism?

EXERCISE: What would it feel like to prove your critics wrong? Describe in detail.

AVOIDING A SHAME SPIRAL

During the five stages of rejection, you may find that one rejection or critique triggers a barrage of negative thoughts and doubts. For example: I got rejected because my idea sucks ➡ That must mean I'm just not talented or smart enough ➡ Of course I'm not smart enough, I did horrible on the SATs ➡ Speaking of SATs, I was such a loser in high school. And I'm a loser now! ➡ I'll never be good at anything, I should just quit.

When you find yourself being needlessly negative or illogically piecing together "proof" of your inadequacy, you're in a shame spiral. One thought leads to another, and just like sinking in quicksand, you'll soon be up to your head in muck. So how do you get out? Here are some tips:

1. *Recognize you are shame spiraling.* Shame spirals begin by linking past rejections or failures together, or letting a rejection color everything bleak: "This day sucks, this week sucks, my life sucks!" When you feel yourself sinking into despair, recognize it's a shame spiral, not the truth.

2. *Relax and breathe deeply.* When you're stuck in quicksand, filling your lungs with air will slow the sinking. If you're freaking out about a rejection or critique, long, slow breaths will calm you down.

3. *Take your time.* Rapid, frantic movements make it hard to escape quicksand. Don't do anything rash after a criticism or rejection. Before making a big decision, give yourself time to feel hurt, angry, or upset.

4. *Use a tool to get out.* Use a revitalizing activity after your shame spiral to boost your spirits and dispel any lingering bad feelings. Find your center with meditation if that's your style, burn off steam with a long run, or lean on your Circle of Trust.

If you wallow in the pain of rejection or criticism for too long, it becomes harder and harder to bounce back. You get two days to feel upset, maximum. After that, you need to take action before you lose all motivation. Let's look at three techniques for dealing with rejection or harsh criticism: Stay, Hit, Fold.

STRATEGY FOR DEALING WITH REJECTION #1:
STAY

"Some people think that success is due to luck
or being in the right place at the right time.
This is simply not true. Successful people
work hard enough and long enough to be
in the right place at the right time."

—Paul Richards, NASA Astronaut

Paul Richards had dreamed of being an astronaut, ever since he was a little boy. After earning an engineering degree, Paul was offered the opportunity of a lifetime: an interview at NASA. Then, tragedy struck—his father passed away. Paul missed his interview to attend the funeral. The next day, he drove to NASA's headquarters only to be told he was too late. There was now a hiring freeze. He watched as his résumé was placed on a huge stack of applications.

Undeterred, Paul spent the next few weeks writing letters to eighty-two different NASA branch heads until someone finally agreed to meet with him. He ended up speaking with the Director of Engineering, who told him, "Son, I took the same approach to get my job here twenty years ago. We have exactly one spot left open, do you want a job?"

Paul took the job as an engineer and kept dreaming of space. He applied to the astronaut-training program and was rejected eight years in a row. His colleagues told him, "Everyone who works here wants to go to space. You'll soon outgrow that idea." Ignoring the naysayers, Paul redoubled his efforts, excelling in his work as an engineer, and created a tool that helped repair the Hubble Space Telescope. In 1995, his ninth application to the astronaut program was accepted. Five years later, Paul watched the sun rise over the Alps—while floating 250 miles above the Earth's surface.

Paul's persistence can be applied to your dream. Don't be ignored. Don't let your résumé get shoved in a file with heaps of others. Follow up, call, write to, and meet with people until you're not just another name on a list.

Find Your Rejection Number

"It takes 99 rejections to have one great victory."

—Kamran Pasha

How much rejection should you expect? Figure it out with online research or read on for suggested rejection numbers from industry veterans. Here are some stories from the trenches:

Comedian/Writer: Thomas Lennon (*Reno 911, Night at the Museum*) has written dozens of screenplays. His movies have made over $1 billion dollars at the box office. He estimates that only 10 percent of what he writes ever progresses beyond his laptop.

"I truly believe that anyone who can write and has a decent sense of humor will produce about 10–14 percent of really good material. The trick is this: you have to write *a lot* (every single day) so that the 10 percent of good material will be large enough for you to earn a living and have success. I hate to say that success is a numbers game, but in many ways, it really is."

—podcast, *Making It with Riki Lindhome*

Fashion Designer: Bliss Lau is an accessories designer with her line in forty stores worldwide. She got her start by taking a train from Washington D.C. to New York, getting off at each stop to visit every boutique store in walking distance. Bliss said, "I got flat-out rejected by half of them and had a great time at only one of them. But the way I saw it, I scored a new client, which was great."

—cnnmoney.com

Freelance Journalist: Kelly James-Enger, the author of *Writer for Hire: 101 Secrets to Freelance Success* said, "Your query may be stellar but it may be rejected for a host of reasons that you have no control over. A query rejection is only of that particular idea, by that particular editor, of that particular magazine. It's not personal. Your best response? Send out a new query to the editor who rejected you, and get that other query out to a market that may be more interested."
 —therenegadewriter.com

Actor: In an interview, actor Liam Neeson said, "For every successful actor, there are countless numbers who don't make it. The name of the game is rejection. You go to an audition and are told you're too tall or you're too Irish or your nose is not quite right. You're rejected for your education, you're rejected for this or that and it's really tough." Some actors say they go through stretches of thirty or forty auditions without a callback. A good goal for a new actor is two to four auditions per week.

Law School: Senior Consultant Laura Dauchy recommends applying to up to thirty schools. Christopher Clough, Prelaw Advisor, recommends the following strategies if the majority or all of your law school applications get rejected:

- Take an LSAT prep course and do everything you can do to get above a 165, which will drastically increase your chances of getting into law school.
- Volunteer or work an entry-level position in the legal field for a year or two. Having real-life experience may result in a law school placing less weight on your GPA and LSAT score.
- Consider a graduate degree that would qualify you for a specialized area of the law—like a public affairs degree (for government-related law) or a technology degree (for patent law).
- Apply to less prestigious schools that are likely to accept you. Once there, work hard and plan a transfer to a more prestigious school after a year or two.
 —virtuallyadvising.com/qa/law20050731cc.html

Chef: Anthony Bourdain, chef, author, and television star, attended culinary school in 1978. Afterwards, he worked his way up the ranks of various kitchens, eventually earning his first Executive Chef position in 1998. The path to Executive Chef took Anthony two decades. A survey on starchefs.com found that the average Executive Chef has been working in the business for twenty years.

Inventor: Thomas Edison filed 1,093 patents in his lifetime. Failure is the nature of the beast when it comes to inventions. A study in *Business Week* estimates that "99.8% of inventions fail to make money . . . Only 3,000 patents out of 1.5 million patents are commercially viable."

Teacher: Some teachers report applying to as many as a hundred jobs and doing around ten interviews before getting an acceptable job offer. Candace Davies from resumes-for-teachers.com recommends contacting ten new schools a day via phone, sending out twenty résumés a day via e-mail, and attending one or two job fairs every month.

Musician: Musicthinktank.com estimates the average band has a 1 in 3,428 chance of being signed to a record deal. Extensive touring, networking, and song-pitching websites (like Sonicbids and SoundCloud) will increase your odds of being heard by an A&R rep.

Nonprofit Fundraiser: Sasha Dichter, Chief Innovation Officer at Acumen Fund, recommends a strategy of 100 rejections a month for fundraising requests. Sasha says: "Here's my pitch: Take one month and get out of the building, knock on every door you can, and promise yourself that you won't stop until you're actually rejected 100 times . . . you'll probably raise the money you need long before you hit 100."

—www.sashadichter.wordpress.com/2012/10/24/one-month-100-rejections

Photographer: Photographer Cole Thompson says: "I have submitted my work to hundreds of shows, exhibitions, and magazines; and while I have gotten in some, I have also received many rejections." Cole says he was able to increase his odds to a 50 percent success rate by: researching photo jurors' personal taste, submitting to exhibitions with less applicants, submitting multiple images to increase his chances, and ensuring that each of his images were drastically different from one another to broaden appeal. Read more: photographyblackwhite.com/rejection

Entrepreneur: Sahar Hashemi says, "When we tried to start up Coffee Republic, we were turned down by nineteen bank managers. The trick is to see rejection as not a big thing, to get used to it, to expect it. It simply represents one person's opinion."

—www.dailymail.co.uk/femail/article-1327598/Why-rejection-good-you

Scientist: Vincent Calcagno, an evolutionary biologist and ecologist, says, "I went through the frustration as a PhD student of having a nice piece of research rejected by five, six, maybe seven journals in a row before it was accepted." Calcagno believes that rejection actually benefits a research paper because "it is improved through multiple rounds of revision and peer editing."

—www.the-scientist.com/?articles.view/articleNo/32787/title/The-Benefits-of-Rejection

Architect: A poster in the archinect.com forums posted the following advice for obtaining an entry-level architecture position in a tough job market: "I called and e-mailed close to 100 firms in Georgia. . . . They all just gave me a generic rejection. I ended up making a pamphlet type portfolio that employers could flip through in about ten seconds and see impressive images. Finally, I just marched from firm to firm (unannounced) and after about three days of this I landed a job. Face time is crucial." Another poster said they had success by including their best two portfolio drawings with their résumé submission.

EXERCISE: Find your rejection number. Do research to see how many rejections newcomers in your field usually go through.

STRATEGY FOR DEALING WITH REJECTION #2:

HIT

If you're experiencing frequent rejection, you may need to change your strategy or alter your goals before you can find success. Let's explore three methods for changing your strategy:

Adjust Your Expectations

Sometimes we get carried away with big expectations of success. You imagine winning an award at Sundance with your first film, scoring a nationwide retail deal for your first clothing line, or getting hired to a leadership position right out of college. It's good to have big goals, but you should also have two or three backup goals. Flexibility is key to success. If Sundance rejects the film, apply to smaller festivals. If a nationwide chain of stores says no, start selling in locally owned shops and boutiques. When you don't score the six-figure salary in your first job interview, start at the bottom and work your way up.

EXERCISE: What are three backup goals if your big plan doesn't pan out?

Edit, Redesign, and Revise

Remember Beatrix Potter's words of wisdom: "The shorter and plainer the better." Often, we are rejected or criticized because we need to go back and rework our product, service, or pitch. To make your work airtight, ask yourself:

- What do you need to simplify or clarify?
- How can you get your message across in less time or space?
- Is it boring? How can you punch it up?
- What's missing?
- How can you highlight the best part(s) of your work?
- How can you make the work more cohesive?

- Is the quality consistent?
- Is your work presented in the most attractive way possible?
- Does it appeal to enough people/customers? How can you appeal to even more?
- Could you make your work more affordable?
- It is it neat and error-free?

EXERCISE: Use the above questions to revise your work.

Don't Wait for Permission

Is someone else truly crucial to achieving your dream? Or can you do it alone? Stop waiting for someone to give you the green light and do it yourself! Self-produce a film instead of letting your screenplay linger in studio limbo. Start your own fantasy football news empire, complete with a podcast, daily blogs, and weekly webisodes. Or, start your own nonprofit.

If the powers-that-be are rejecting or ignoring you, find a way to be successful without them. If you make a big enough splash, they won't be able to ignore you for much longer. As comedian Jonathan Winters said: "If your ship doesn't come in, swim out to meet it!" The industry you want to break into is already full. Just like an exclusive club, they rarely invite outsiders to the party. No one wants to let the new kid in, especially a new kid with little credibility, prestige, or experience. Stop waiting for an invite. Start your own club. Many successful people have ripped up their rejection slips and taken a do-it-yourself approach to their dreams:

Mindy Kaling tried to break into comedy by writing pilots for sitcoms. After dozens of sample scripts and no job offers, she decided to write, act in, and direct a two-person off-Broadway comedy show with her roommate. From that success, she was offered a job to write and star in *The Office*.

When Joan Jett went solo, she tried to get a record label to distribute her new album. She was rejected by twenty-three different companies. Out of frustration, she founded Blackheart Records with producer Kenny Laguna in 1980 and released the solo album herself.

Barton Brooks wanted to get rid of the bureaucracy and red tape associated with international aid work, so he started a one-man organization called Guerrilla Aid. Barton travels the globe, on a budget of $20 a day, working with community members to lay bricks, build wells, plant trees, and deliver donated clothing, wheelchairs, and chickens.

EXERCISE: What would a do-it-yourself approach look like for you?

STRATEGY FOR DEALING WITH REJECTION #3:
FOLD

When is it appropriate to give up on a project? Here are some hints that it may be time to move on:

- Long-gone dream: Are you 100 percent sure you have no passion left for this dream? Would you have no regrets if you moved on?
- Ethical conflict: Are you being asked to do something that makes you uncomfortable, goes against your values, or is wrong for your community?
- Dangerous dream: Are you emotionally, physically, or financially damaging yourself or your loved ones?
- Bad investment: Are you drowning in debt or sinking your money into something with no pay back?
- Start planning an exit strategy if the following is true: You've surpassed your rejection number and then some, lowered your expectations multiple times, changed your strategy multiple times, and lost all motivation and don't want to get it back.

Signs Your Business May Be in Trouble

Sales are consistently slowing down. If sales keep declining, despite all your best efforts, it might be a failing business.

Your losses are increasing. After your initial investment, you should have a steady climb towards profitability.

You are failing to raise more money. It's not a great sign if the people who used to lend money are now backing out. When banks, investors, or friends are all telling you no, it's a sign to get out.

You're starting to owe more than you own. Most people need to borrow money to start a business or launch a creative career. That's fine. But, if the percent of what you owe as compared to what you own is on the rise, it's usually a sign that things are headed downhill.

You've resorted to credit to fund your business. If you're maxing out credit cards to pay for business expenses, it is probably time to implement an exit strategy.

Plan Your Exit Strategy

If you feel ready to abandon a project, there are a few steps you need to take before moving on:

1. Wrap up any loose ends. Be sure to take care of any outstanding paperwork, debts, legal obligations, contracts, or assets you need to sell.

2. Talk to anyone involved in your dream, thank them for their work, and let them know about your decision to move on. If you are working closely with a partner or team, your decision to fold might need to be a group choice. Give advanced warning to partners or employees so they have time to plot their next steps.

3. Come up with a plan for the future. Ask your network if they know about any new opportunities or jobs. Have something in the works as you begin dissolving your old project.

EXERCISE: No matter where you are in your journey, it's smart to always have an exit strategy. Answer the following: What is your exit plan? How will you wrap up all loose ends, recoup any financial investments, and make your next move?

CREATING YOUR OWN LUCK

Notice that none of our advice is "get lucky." Success is almost never a result of luck. Our high school friend, Greg Merson, is a professional poker player. Greg has played over 7 million hands of poker in his life, averaging 2 million hands a year. Fellow poker player Christian Harder said, "From 2007–2010, Greg played as many hands online as anyone in the world. He's a huge grinder and such a huge worker." In 2012, the work paid off. Greg won the World Series of Poker Main Event for $8.53 million dollars and was named Poker Player of the Year.

Poker might be a game of luck but Greg's story proves that anyone can increase their chances for success with good old-fashioned hard work and practice. Dream opportunities are not given by chance, they are fought for and won. You need to be willing to out-work and outlast everyone else. Find your equivalent to 7 million hands of poker, and put in the work.

SUMMARY POINTS

- Expect frequent rejection. Allow time for the Five Stages of Rejection/Criticism before reacting.

- Don't linger more than two days on a rejection or criticism. Take action. Survive the shame spiral.

- Dreams are built with persistence. Find your rejection number.

- If you're frequently rejected, adjust your expectations, revise, or take a do-it-yourself approach.

- Learn to let go of projects that are dead-ends.

- Make your own luck.

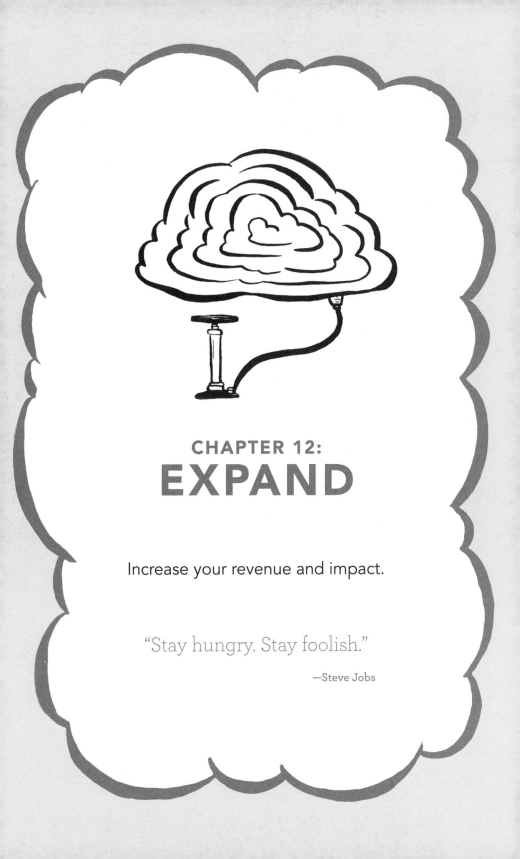

CHAPTER 12:
EXPAND

Increase your revenue and impact.

"Stay hungry. Stay foolish."

—Steve Jobs

Big breaks don't happen overnight but they do happen. After fifty submissions, someone agrees to publish your graphic novel. After six internships and endless networking events, someone offers you your overseas dream job. After two years of fighting to end disease in an underdeveloped nation, you get the funding you need to put boots on the ground and make a real impact. These are turning points in our lives; when the countless crazed hours of work finally pay off. Now let's talk about expanding on a big break, finding new revenue streams, and creating lasting success. We will cover the following:

1. The Three C's of Success
2. Giving Back
3. Letting Nothing Go to Waste
4. Knowledge is Power . . . And Money
5. Finding and Executing the Next Project

THE THREE C'S OF SUCCESS

Today, people want it all: to earn a living, love their work, and do good for the world. This new definition of success has three components:

Contentment: Intrinsic enjoyment in daily work

Contribution: Giving back or improving the world

Cash: Financial well being

EXERCISE: Describe the current state of The Three C's in your life. Answer the following:

- How content do you feel with your work? How can you increase your satisfaction?
- Do you feel like you are contributing to your community or society? What are your goals for contributing more?
- How are you doing financially? What are your financial goals?

EXERCISE: Make three or more action items you can take to better meet your goals for each of the three C's.

GIVING BACK

The lines between work, purpose, and doing good are beginning to blur. Activism, sustainability, and social responsibility are becoming fundamental parts of the new career model. What can you do to contribute to the greater good? Could you . . . donate a portion of your proceeds? Donate your space? Host an event for a charity? Offer your goods or services for free to people who can't afford to pay? Or, become a mentor and offer your time or connections to a newbie? Wealth has more value when shared. If you have been lucky enough to pursue your dream, lend a helping hand to those less fortunate or just starting out.

Kyle Berner, founder of Feelgoodz Flip Flops, operates with a triple bottom-line philosophy: People, Planet, Profit. His flip-flops are made with all-natural Thai rubber, ethically farmed on a co-op. The rubber is sold according to the fair market rate to ensure the farmers earn a comfortable living. At the manufacturing plants in Thailand and Vietnam, the workers are paid a higher-than-average wage, offered health insurance, provided transportation, and included in company events like the annual tennis tournaments. Once created, the flip-flops are shipped to American markets using UPS Carbon Neutral. After the customer's flip-flops are wearing thin, they can be chopped up and buried in a garden— Feelgoodz are completely biodegradable.

EXERCISE: How can you incorporate the People, Planet, Profit philosophy into your work?

LETTING NOTHING GO TO WASTE

Byproducts and leftover materials can be recycled, repurposed, and monetized. The 16 Mile Brewery in Delaware sells off the useful byproducts of the brewing process to local farmers and artisans to create livestock feed, gourmet bread, and cheese. Other careers can have profitable leftovers too. A photographer takes two-hundred photos, sells ten to a magazine, and puts another fifty up for sale on a stock photo website. A restaurant owner rents out their place to host meetings and parties during non-peak hours. A computer technician uses spare parts to fix gaming consoles at night for a small fee, of course.

EXERCISE: What can you reuse, repurpose, or recycle for a profit? List three things.

KNOWLEDGE IS POWER . . . AND MONEY

You can also create an additional revenue stream by sharing your knowledge and experiences. Your words can inspire, educate, and make an impact. Tap into your inner How-to Guru. If you've overcome obstacles, share how you did it. Write tutorials about harnessing social media for profit, blog about how you got an investor, or create YouTube tutorials for changing a website header. If you could have used the help on your journey, so could someone else.

Hard-to-find or poorly organized information also presents a money-making opportunity. Do you wish there were more books, e-books, first-hand accounts, websites, articles, podcasts, PDF guides, or tutorials about certain aspects of your dream? Once you've found some success, you are qualified to fill these knowledge gaps. Share the info for a price or sign up advertisers. The profit may be small at first, but it can add up. More importantly, you'll start to become known for your expertise.

EXERCISE: Make a list of everything you've learned about your dream so far. Be sure to include technical, miscellaneous, or industry-specific details. Who would benefit from this information? How can you share it?

Teach. Consult. Coach.

Do you have a gift for drumming up publicity? Can you help someone clean up their business plan? Or can you offer time management skills and tools? Now that you have experience in your chosen field, your advice can have a price. Share your know-how by creating an online class and charging a fee for registration. Or, teach a seminar at your local community center or college. Another cash cow? Coach individuals for an hourly or flat fee. Be specific about the services you offer and advertise on your website, through word of mouth, and social media.

EXERCISE: What would you teach? Make an outline for a class or coaching session.

Telling the Story

People love to be inspired and informed by successful dream-chasers. If you enjoy sharing your story, you can earn extra revenue with public-speaking engagements at schools, conferences, or corporate functions.

Blogger Caitlin Boyle took this approach after publishing her book, *Operation Beautiful*. Her story? One night before class, feeling overwhelmed and stressed out, Caitlin decided she wanted to do something nice for somebody else. She stuck a Post-It note on the mirror in her community college's bathroom with the message: "You are beautiful. You are good enough the way you are." She took a photo of the note, posted it on her popular healthy-living blog, and asked her readers to participate and send in photos of their own notes.

Responses poured in and Caitlin launched the website operationbeautiful.com to share all of the inspiring notes. Two months later, Operation Beautiful was featured in the *New York Daily News* and a month after that she was offered a book deal. Caitlin has expanded on her success by touring the country to speak with young women about self-esteem.

EXERCISE: Craft your story. Write an outline for a lecture or workshop you would like to give.

EXERCISE: Identify three groups that would benefit from hearing your story. How would you reach them?

FINDING THE NEXT PROJECT

The key to lasting success is innovation; living with one foot in the present and one in the future. A writer needs the next story, a painter needs a blank canvas, a marketing executive needs the next campaign. Once you've reached one mountaintop, you're ready to conquer the next summit.

After being so immersed in your first project, you may become stuck in your ways and develop tunnel vision. If you're looking for your next idea, search in unfamiliar territory. Take a brief vacation, travel somewhere you've never been, read something new, talk to a stranger, and try activities that pique your curiosity. Inspiration can come easily when we are engrossed in something strange or exotic.

Get lost in brainstorming ideas, taking notes, sketching, researching a thought-provoking issue you love, or recording ideas on tape or film. New ideas need time to germinate and flower. Whatever you do, don't force it. Instead of desperately seeking out the next big project, relax and reflect on your journey. What have you learned? How have you grown? Renew your daily reflection techniques: meditation, journaling, walking, running, exercising, cooking, or driving. These activities will settle the mind, give you fresh perspective, and sow the seeds for a new idea.

Real World Examples of Expansion Projects

- Scott Shuffitt, the founder of *Lebowski Fest* we discussed in chapter 1, has expanded on his love for movies by creating his own film, *Bricks and Mortar and Love*, about the struggles of his local indie record shop.
- Mokotsi Rukundo, the CorNroc food cart entrepreneur we discussed in chapter 3, has expanded by creating Moto Hot Sauce, based on his grandma's tongue-sizzling recipe.
- Chinaka Hodge got her start in poetry, performing on two seasons of HBO's *Def Poetry*. Later, she expanded to the narrative format, writing a play called *Mirrors in Every Corner*, which received rave reviews. Chinaka is currently chasing her next big dream of being a screenwriter.
- Megan McJames, an Olympic skier we spoke with in Park City, Utah, told us that after retiring from professional competition, she hopes to open a bakery called the Finish Line in a ski town.
- Kirk Coco, a craft brewer we met in New Orleans, started his business by producing kegs for local bars. He has since expanded by bottling his beer and selling to the tri-state area.

EXERCISE: Make a bucket list of things you want to do before you die. Could any of the activities on the list lead to your next passion project?

When to Tackle New Projects and Products as a Business

How can you invent a new product or service line without detracting from your core business? Here are some tips:

You should be turning a profit and feel financially comfortable before taking on a new project. Wait until you're through the start-up phase of your business. The time to expand is when everything is running smoothly, you feel in control, and your current business is relatively low maintenance.

Businesses require a lot of time and attention. Can you outsource any tasks to put your business on autopilot before tackling new endeavors? Can you hire a general manager so you have more time to work on the next expansion?

If your new idea is unrelated to your current business, consider cashing out before you tackle a new project. Find a purchaser for your business and sell. This can fund your next move and free up your time. For example, web entrepreneur and inventor Zach Kaplan sold his first website, took a trip to Disney Land to get inspired, and then started his second website, inventables.com.

EXECUTING THE NEXT PROJECT

Once you have a new idea, get ready to start all over again with a new step-by-step plan, saving money, fundraising, and dealing with your old pals—fear of failure, risk, and rejection. The dreamer's journey is a continuous circle of thrilling ideas, the challenge of execution, the sting of rejection, and the sweet taste of success.

The Dreamer's Journey

Years ago, Alex Reymundo was holding down two jobs: a salesman-by-day to pay the bills, and a stand-up comic by night to fuel his passion for laughter and entertainment. The financial pressures were on, Alex's wife was pregnant, and his bosses were trying to motivate him to make more sales. At a staff meeting, his boss told him, "A man who chases two rabbits, will never eat." That night, Alex's wife told him to chase the rabbit he loved: comedy. After that, Alex committed himself to comedy full-time. Within a year, he was touring with comedian Paul Rodriguez. This led to the opportunity of a lifetime: Alex was offered a spot on a special called *The Original Latin Kings of Comedy*, featuring comedians like George Lopez, Cheech Marin, and Joey Medina.

The Original Latin Kings of Comedy was a big break, but Alex knew lasting success would require another huge risk. He decided to fund and create his own one-hour special. "My manager and I took out some money, mortgaged our homes, and found a couple investors," Alex said. "We gambled everything. A few days before the special we had only sold fifty-six tickets. It was terrifying; I really began to have doubts. We worked our asses off to sell more tickets—

going to every radio station, TV station, chamber of commerce meeting, and luncheon. I even worked a McDonald's Drive-Thru just for the press," Alex said. The effort paid off and the show sold out. Showtime and Comedy Central both bought the rights to air the special, earning Alex all of his money back.

Alex summed up the life cycle of a dreamer: "I can't rest. It doesn't matter what you did last year. All that matters is what you are doing now. Successful people always have their next project in the works." And so, the dreamer's journey goes on, a continuous cycle of reaching one horizon and setting sail for the next. Keep dreaming, keep striving, and don't forget to enjoy the ride. We believe in you. Good luck and share this book with others you meet on the dreamer's journey!

ACKNOWLEDGMENTS

Rick Benzel, this book wouldn't exist without your support and guidance. We'd like to thank our wonderful literary agents, Steve Harris and Michele Martin. You believed in us and it changed our lives. We also thank our editor, Cindy De La Hoz, and the great team at Running Press who made our dream for a book come to life.

Kathy Eldon, Joey Borgogna, and everyone at the Creative Visions Foundation, you are miracle workers. Thank you for mentoring us along our journey. We are also blessed to have amazing friends and family—thank you for the love, support, and encouragement. You guys are the best!

Finally, we are forever grateful to everyone who helped us fund and create *The Dream Share Project* film, especially the dreamers who agreed to be interviewed. Thanks for taking a chance on two kids with Flip cams. Your advice, wisdom, and stories have inspired countless people across the country.

 NOTES

NOTES

NOTES

NOTES

 NOTES

NOTES

NOTES

NOTES